OZ *Clarke's*

INTRODUCING

WINE

WEBSTERS

LITTLE, BROWN AND COMPANY
BOSTON NEW YORK LONDON

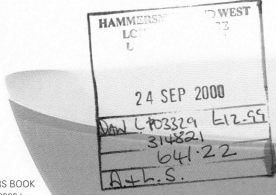

A LITTLE, BROWN/WEBSTERS BOOK
This edition first published in 2000 by
Little, Brown and Company (UK)
Brettenham House, Lancaster Place,
London WC2E 7EN

Created and designed by
Websters International Publishers Limited,
Axe and Bottle Court, 70 Newcomen Street,
London SE1 1YT
www.websters.co.uk
www.ozclarke.com

A CIP catalogue for this book is available from the British Library
ISBN 0 316 85450 6

Corporate Sales
Companies, institutions and other organisations wishing to make bulk
purchases of this or any other Oz Clarke title published by Little, Brown
should contact the Special Sales Department on +44(0)20-7911 8089.

Acknowledgements
Thanks to Vinopolis, City of Wine and Michael Johnson Ceramics for the
loan of Riedel wine glasses and other items for photography; Roberson
wine merchants, London for the picture of their shop on page 66; Spiral
Cellars for the picture on page 67; and to Zaika, London for the restaurant
picture on page 59. Thanks also to Fiona Holman, Nigel O'Gorman and
Andrew Thompson for their kind assistance in preparing this book.

Editor Bill Evans
Art Editor Emma Ashby
Consultant Editor Margaret Rand
Photography Mick Rock/Cephas Picture Library, Robert Hall,
    Stephen Bartholomew, Stephen Marwood; see page 144 for
    full picture credits
Editorial Director Claire Harcup
Indexer Marie Lorimer
Production Kâren Connell
Colour reproduction by Pixel Tech PTE Ltd, Singapore
Printed and bound by Edições ASA S.A., Portugal

Prices of recommended wines
The price bands for the wines recommended on
pages 76–137 correspond to the following
sterling prices for a standard 750ml bottle. Prices
are intended for guidance only and may vary.

① under £5		② £5–£10		③ £10–£15
④ £15–£20		⑤ over £20		

314821

Contents

Next time you walk into a wine shop, stop for a moment and have a good look around. Don't head straight for this month's special offer, don't blinker your vision to everything but your trusty favourites, just have a good gawp at the whole range that's on display. If the shop is big and you're anything like me, your head will start to spin and the overwhelming abundance of different wines will leave you dizzy with delight. Imagine it – there's a unique flavour stoppered up in every one of those bottles. So open your mind, pick a bottle, any bottle, and head off on a lifetime's joyous voyage of discovery.

But is it really worth making the effort to know the difference between all those bottles on the shelf? Oh yes! Yes, yes and yes again. Just a little knowledge will double the pleasure you get from a glass of wine and will give you the key to choosing wines that you like. And if a little knowledge can give you that, does a little more knowledge sound attractive? That's why this book is here, to help you look beyond those special offers and trusty favourites – to help you discover for yourself a world of new, exciting and delicious flavours.

Are you ready? Then get reading, get shopping and start enjoying yourself!

Part 1

The Flavours of Wine

When you buy wine, buy it for its flavour. Reputation, packaging and price all vie to influence your choice, but they can't titillate your tastebuds. The grape variety used is the most significant factor in determining the taste of a wine, but everything that happens to the grapes and their juice on the long journey from the vine to the glass in your hand contributes to that wine's unique identity. Read on and start getting the flavour you want.

Get the flavour you want

YOUR CHANCES OF walking into a wine shop and coming out with a wine that's enjoyable to drink, whatever the price level, are better now than ever before. The last quarter of the 20th century saw a revolution in wine, in terms of both style and quality.

All wines are cleaner and fresher-tasting than they were; reds are juicier, rounder and softer; whites are more tropical, more peachy-ripe. There are more new oak barrels being used, which in terms of taste means vanilla and buttered toast. Which isn't to say that all wines taste alike. Indeed, there's never been a wider choice. It's just that modern winemaking is rapidly eliminating faults – it's not eliminating individuality.

So how do you choose? How do you tell a wine that's just right for summer lunch in the garden from one that would be better suited to a winter evening in front of a log fire? Well, imagine if when you walked into that wine shop you could pick up a bottle from the 'green, tangy white' shelf or go for a 'spicy, warm-hearted red'. That would make things pretty easy, wouldn't it?

You see, all those thousands of different flavours fall into the 15 broad styles shown here and which I describe in detail over the next few pages. So, even if you don't yet know a thing about grape varieties and wine-producing regions, just choose a style that appeals and I'll point you in the right direction. And come back to these pages whenever you fancy something new – I'll do my best to set you off on a whole new flavour adventure.

1. Juicy, fruity

Refreshing, approachable and delicious – Chilean Merlot shows what modern red wine is all about

2. Silky, strawberryish

Mellow, perfumed wine with red fruit flavours – Pinot Noir is the classic grape

3. Intense, blackcurranty

Reds with the distinctive blackcurrant flavour of Cabernet Sauvignon

6. Delicate rosé

Fragrant, refreshing and dry – good ones come from Provence and Navarra

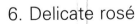

4. Spicy, warm-hearted

Gloriously rich flavours of fruit berries, black pepper and chocolate – try Aussie Shiraz

5. Mouthwatering, sweet-sour

Intriguing wines with a rasping herby bite and sweet-sour red fruit flavours – Italian reds do this better than any

7. Bone-dry, neutral

Crisp, refreshing wines like Muscadet and Verdicchio

8. Green, tangy

Sharp, gooseberryish New Zealand Sauvignon Blanc leads the way

9. Intense, nutty

Rich and succulent, subtle and powerful – white Burgundy sets the style

10. Ripe, toasty

Upfront flavours of peaches, apricots and tropical fruits with toasty richness – the taste of Aussie Chardonnay

11. Aromatic

Perfumy wines with exotic and floral fragrances – none more so than Gewürztraminer

12. Sparkling

Bubbles to make you happy and delicious flavours, too. Smile, you're drinking Champagne

13. Golden, sweet

Luscious mouthfuls with intense flavours of peach, apricot and honey, such as Sauternes

14. Warming

Sweet fortified wines with rich flavours – nothing beats port

15. Tangy, fortified

Bone dry with startling stark, sour and nutty flavours – this is real sherry

1. Juicy, fruity reds

Lots of fruit flavour makes for tasty, refreshing reds ideal for gulping down with or without food. This is the definitive modern style for the best cheap red wines and those one step up at the delicious-yet-affordable level, emphasising fruit flavour and minimising the gum-drying toughness of tannin.

This style had its birth in the New World – you'll find it in wines from Australia, California, Washington State, New Zealand, South America and South Africa – but it has spread right through Europe, overturning any lingering ideas that red wine must be aged. You don't age these wines. You buy them and you drink them. And then you buy some more. For juicy, fruity flavours, don't even look at a wine that's more than about two years old.

Chilean Merlot is the benchmark for this worldwide phenomenon: young, well-balanced, and bursting with blackberry, blackcurrant and plum flavours.

Spain produces lots of inexpensive soft, supple reds in the same mould. Anything from La Mancha, Navarra or Valdepeñas is worth a try. California does a nice line in young Merlots and Zinfandels and Argentina has smooth Tempranillo, ultra-fruity Bonarda and juicy Malbec.

If you want French wine, Beaujolais is famous for this style, though it tends to be a bit pricier and a bit less obviously fruity than you might hope; Vin de Pays d'Oc reds are often a better bet.

THE BUILDING BLOCKS OF WINE

All wines have some basic elements in common:

Acid and sugar are present in the juice of the grape. The sugar is turned into alcohol during fermentation, but some can remain. A lot of leftover sugar makes for a sweet wine. Acid sounds unpleasant and aggressive, but when present in the right proportion it makes the wine intense and refreshing. All wines contain acid, just as all fruits do.

Tannin comes from the skins, stems and pips of the grape. This is the stuff in red wines that stains your teeth and dries your mouth, but in the right amounts can do marvellous things to the flavour and texture of the wine. White wines don't have noticeable levels of tannin. Tannin and acid both have the added benefit of acting as preservatives, and wines with high levels of either (or both) have the potential to last for many years in the bottle.

Alcohol, the reason many of us started drinking wine in the first place, isn't just there for the sake of getting you lit up. It balances other flavours, for example softening the attack of the acid, and contributes to the intensity of the experience of the wine in your mouth.

2. Silky, strawberryish reds

Mellow, perfumed reds with a gentle strawberry, raspberry or cherry fruit fragrance and flavour. Good ones feel silky in your mouth.

Pinot Noir is the grape that produces the supreme examples of this style. Great Pinot Noir has a silkiness of texture no other grape can emulate. Only a few regions make it well and the good stuff is expensive.

Pinot Noir's home territory, and the place where it achieves greatness, is Burgundy in France (Bourgogne in French). Virtually all red Burgundy is made from Pinot Noir. The best wines mature to develop aromas of truffles, game and decaying autumn leaves – sounds horrible, I know, but just one taste is enough to get some people hooked for life.

Beyond Burgundy the best Pinot Noir comes from California, particularly in Carneros and Santa Barbara, from Oregon and from New Zealand.

Cheap Pinot Noir is rarely good, but Chile's usually have loads of vibrant jellied fruit flavour. Somontano in Spain has some tasty budget examples, too.

Red Rioja and Navarra, also from Spain but made from different grapes, are soft and smooth with a fragrant strawberryish quality. This also appears in the lightest Côtes du Rhône-Villages from France. None of these wines, however, has the silkiness of Pinot Noir.

3. Intense, blackcurranty reds

Full-flavoured red wines with firm tannins and a distinctive blackcurrant flavour. They're made from Cabernet Sauvignon alone or blended with Merlot and other grapes to enrich the fruit flavours and soften the texture.

Cabernet Sauvignon is the grape to look for here. The Cabernet-based red wines of Bordeaux in France are the original blackcurranty wines with, at their best, a fragrance of cigar boxes and lead pencils. New World Cabernets have more blackcurrant, but also a vanillary flavour and sometimes mint. It's hard to know who's ahead on quality at the top. At the less expensive end it's perfectly obvious: the New World wins almost every time. The cheapest red Bordeaux is joyless stuff.

Nevertheless, Cabernet Sauvignon is one of the most reliable wines you can get. It retains its characteristic flavours wherever it's from, and at every price level – and that's rare in wine. Expensive ones should be ripe and rich with layers of intense flavour: cheaper ones have simpler flavours that are more earthy, more jammy, or more green-pepper lean.

For budget Cabernets, check out Bulgaria, Chile, Australia, South Africa and France's Vins de Pays d'Oc. If you want to pay a bit more, try Penedès in Spain, Australia again, Chile again, South Africa again, and Bordeaux or its better-value neighbour, Bergerac.

You'll also find these blackcurrant flavours in Ribera del Duero from Spain, although the grape here is Tempranillo.

Red wine wheel

Here's another way to get the flavour you want. I've arranged the world's red wines according to their intensity and the broad type of flavour. The wines at the outer edge have layer upon layer of flavour; those near the centre are light and simple.

Black fruits Blackcurrant, blackberry, dark plum and black cherry flavours.

Red fruits The soft flavours of strawberries and raspberries and sharper hints of redcurrants and red cherries.

Herbs/spices The wild flavours of herbs; peppery and aromatic spices; and tastes such as chocolate or liquorice.

Wine flavours

Increasing intensity

KEY
The styles I have described in this chapter fit the zones of the wheel like this:

Juicy, fruity reds RED FRUITS or BLACK FRUITS, with light to medium intensity

Silky, strawberryish reds RED FRUITS, though the most intense have a shade of BLACK FRUITS, too.

Intense, blackcurranty reds BLACK FRUITS, maybe with a touch of RED FRUITS or HERBS/SPICES.

Spicy, warm-hearted reds HERBS/SPICES, but many combine this with RED FRUITS or BLACK FRUITS.

Mouthwatering, sweet-sour reds RED FRUITS and HERBS/SPICES.

BLACK FRUITS

top Californian Cabernet Sauvignon

top Australian Cabernet Sauvignon

top Washington Cabernet
and Merlot

top Bordeaux from St-Emilion and Pomerol

top Pessac-Léognan

top Bordeaux from the Médoc

Ribera del Duero

top Chilean and South African Cabernet Sauvignon

top Argentine Malbec

top Chilean Merlot

BLACK FRUITS AND HERBS/SPICES

BLACK AND RED FRUITS

mid-priced Australian Cabernet Sauvignon

mid-priced Californian Cabernet Sauvignon · New Zealand Merlot

top Australian Shiraz

mid-priced Argentine Malbec

Douro

Navarra

mid-priced South African Cabernet Sauvignon

top Loire reds (Chinon, Bourgueil, Saumur-Champigny)

big Zinfandel

hefty Pinotage

South African Shiraz

southern Portuguese reds

New Zealand Cabernet Sauvignon

Loire reds (Chinon, Bourgueil, Saumur Champigny)

mid-priced Argentine Shiraz

light Australian Shiraz

mid-priced Bordeaux
(crus bourgeois)

Bulgarian Cabernet
Sauvignon

Hungarian reds

Côte-Rôtie

Priorat

Toro

Coteaux du Languedoc and
Côtes du Roussillon

Penedès

cheap Chilean Cabernet
and Merlot

North Italian Merlot

light Rioja

Beaujolais crus

Premier and Grand Cru Burgundy

Hermitage

California Syrah and Mourvèdre

Valdepeñas and
La Mancha

Australian Pinot Noir
Chilean and South African
Pinot Noir

New Zealand and Californian Pinot Noir

Mexican Petite Sirah

Fitou

Minervois

Austrian reds

LIGHT AND SIMPLE

LIGHT AND SIMPLE

cheap Bordeaux

New York Pinot Noir

Oregon Pinot Noir

good Burgundy

Cornas

Crozes-Hermitage and St-Joseph

Cahors

Chianti Classico

light Italian reds

cheap German reds

light Pinotage

Argentine Tempranillo

top Rioja Reserva and Gran Reserva

HERBS/SPICES

Dão and
Bairrada

Valpolicella
Classico

cheap
Burgundy
and Beaujolais

simple
and Beaujolais · basic vins de pays

Côtes du Rhône

Costières de Nîmes

light Chianti

RED FRUITS

Brunello di Montalcino

Dolcetto

Corbières

Barbera

mid-priced Zinfandel

Provence reds (e.g. Bandol)

Vin de pays Cabernet and Merlot

Barbaresco

Chianti Classico Riserva and Vino Nobile di Montepulciano

southern Italian reds

Côtes du Rhône-Villages

Barolo

Vacqueyras

Grenache

Australian old vines

Gigondas and

Châteauneuf-du-Pape

RED FRUITS AND HERBS/SPICES

4. Spicy, warm-hearted reds

Dense, heartwarming, gloriously rich flavours of fruit berries, black pepper and chocolate, ideal for winter evenings or barbecues. The leading grape variety is known either as Syrah or Shiraz.

Australian Shiraz is the wine to try: dense, rich and chocolaty, sometimes with a twist of pepper, sometimes with a whiff of smoke, sometimes with a slap of leather. You can get good examples at all price levels.

In France's Rhône Valley the same grape is known as Syrah, and of course it was grown here long before the Aussies got their hands on it. Rhône Syrah tends to be a little more austere in style, and smoky-minerally to Australia's rich spice. It's more expensive, too.

For good value from France try Vin de Pays d'Oc Syrah, Fitou, Minervois or heavier styles of Côtes du Rhône-Villages (lighter ones are more in the silky, strawberryish style).

Portugal offers good value with a whole host of indigenous grape varieties found nowhere else. In Spain, try the weighty plums and vanilla flavours of Toro and the more expensive Priorat.

California Zinfandel made in its most powerful style is spicy and rich. In South America, Mexican Petite Sirah is not the Syrah grape, but it's wonderfully earthy and rich. Warming Argentine Malbecs and Chile's great big spicy-savoury mouthfuls of Carmenère are excellent value. Take a look at South African Pinotage, too.

Wine terms | Oak

If wine is fermented or matured in oak barrels, it will acquire characteristic oak flavours from the wooden staves, particularly if the winemaker chooses brand new, fairly small barrels called **barriques**. Wine tasters describe these **new oak** flavours as toastiness, spiciness, butteriness, butterscotch and vanilla. Many of the world's best reds and whites are fermented or matured in oak, but stainless steel or concrete tanks, which don't affect the flavour, are preferable for fresh-tasting and ultra-fruity styles.

5. Mouthwatering, sweet-sour reds

Intriguing wines with sweet-sour cherry and plum fruit flavours and a rasping herby bite. These wines almost all hail from Italy and have a character that's distinctly different from the international mob.

It must be something to do with the Italian taste in wine. There's a rasp of sourness in these reds that's intended to cut through steak or duck, not be sipped as an apéritif. You'll find that same irresistible sour-cherries edge on wines made from all sorts of grapes – Dolcetto, Sangiovese, Barbera – and in wines from Chianti to the rare but lip-smacking Teroldego. Some have a delicious raisiny taste, too. Even light, low-tannin Valpolicella has this characteristic Italian flavour when it's good.

Up in Piedmont, tough, tannic wines from Barolo, made from the stern Nebbiolo grape, have a fascinating tar-and-roses flavour. Good Barolo is frighteningly expensive these days, but a decent Langhe will give you the flavour for less money. Down in the South, there's a whole raft of reds, such as Copertino and Salice Salentino, which add round, pruny flavours to the sour-cherry bite. Sicilian reds are good news, too.

California grows quite a bit of Sangiovese, but somehow it seldom has the same stylishness. Argentina makes tasty wine from several Italian grape varieties.

6. Delicate rosé

Good rosé should be fragrant and refreshing, and deliciously dry – not sickly and sweet.

People always apologise for liking rosé – why? It's lovely stuff: dry, strawberryish, perhaps herby, and ideal for summer drinking and with lots of vegetable dishes.

The best grape for rosé is Grenache, but it's by no means the only suitable one. Provence and other parts of southern France make good rosé; so do Bordeaux, Navarra in Spain and Portugal. But rosé can come from anywhere really. the Loire's Rosé d'Anjou is generally one to avoid; Cabernet d'Anjou is usually better, and drier. Blush Zinfandel from California is fairly sweet, but okay.

7. Bone-dry, neutral whites

Crisp, refreshing whites whose flavours won't set the world alight – but chill them down and set them next to a plate of shellfish and you've got the perfect combination.

These wines may not sound very enticing, but there are plenty of occasions when you just don't want to be hit over the palate with oak and tropical fruit.

In France, Muscadet from the Loire Valley is the most neutral of the lot. Unoaked Chablis from Burgundy is the adaptable Chardonnay grape in a dry, minerally style.

Italy specialises in this sort of wine, because Italians don't really like their white wines to be aromatic. So Frascati, most Soave, Orvieto, Verdicchio, Lugana, Pinot Grigio, Pinot Bianco and Chardonnay from the Alto Adige all fit the bill.

You won't find this style in the New World – winemakers there don't want neutrality in their wines. Even when they grow the same vines (and mostly they don't) they make fuller, more flavoursome wines from them.

8. Green, tangy whites

Sharp, zesty, love-them-or-hate-them wines, often with the smell and taste of gooseberries.

Sauvignon Blanc from New Zealand – especially from Marlborough – has tangy, mouthwatering flavours by the bucketful. Chile makes similar, slightly softer wines, South African versions can have real bite and Spain uses it to give Rueda some extra zip.

Sancerre and Pouilly-Fumé from the Loire Valley in France are crisp and refreshing with lighter fruit flavours and a minerally or even a smoky edge. Vin de Pays du Jardin de la France offers similar flavours at lower prices.

The biggest bargain in Sauvignon Blanc is dry white Bordeaux. It's generally labelled as Bordeaux Sauvignon Blanc or maybe Bordeaux Blanc, and standards have risen out of sight in recent years. It's always softer than Loire or New Zealand versions.

The Loire also produces sharp-edged wines from Chenin Blanc, such as Vouvray and Savennières. Loire Chenin has a minerally acid bite when young, but becomes rich and honeyed with age.

Riesling is the other grape to look out for here. Rieslings are peachy, minerally and smoky when young, with a streak of green apple and some high-tensile acidity. With a few years' bottle age those flavours mingle and mellow to a wonderful honeyed, petrolly flavour – sounds disgusting, tastes heavenly. The leanest, often with a touch of sweetness to balance the acidity, come from Germany's Mosel Valley; slightly richer ones come from the Rhine; drier, weightier ones from Austria and Alsace. Australian Rieslings, both dry and sweet, have an irresistible limes-and-toast flavour.

9. Intense, nutty whites

Rich and succulent whites with subtle nut and oatmeal flavours. These wines are generally oak-aged and have a soft edge with a backbone of absolute dryness.

If you like this style, you've got a taste for French classics, because the best expression of it is oak-aged Chardonnay in the form of white Burgundy. This is the wine that earned Chardonnay its renown in the first place and the style is sometimes matched in the best examples from California, New York State, New Zealand, Australia and South Africa. Not any old examples, mind you – just the best. Italian producers in Tuscany are having a go, too.

Top-quality oak-aged Graves and Pessac-Léognan from Bordeaux are Sémillon blended with Sauvignon Blanc, giving a creamy, nutty wine with a hint of nectarines. Unoaked Australian Semillon (note the 'unoaked' – it means it hasn't been aged in oaked barrels) from the Hunter Valley matures to become waxy and rich. The best white Rioja from Spain, too, becomes nutty and lush with time.

None of these wines comes cheap and they all need time to show their best. Less costly alternatives which give an idea of the style are Spanish Chardonnays from Navarra and Somontano.

 Wine terms | **Varietals and blends**

A wine made solely or principally from a single grape variety is known as a **varietal**. These wines are often named after the relevant grape. This is the simple, modern way to label wine and I'm all in favour, because it is the particular grape variety which contributes most strongly to the flavour. The law in the country or region of production specifies the minimum percentage of the grape that the wine must contain to be given a varietal name. A **blend** made from two or more varieties does not signify an inferior wine: on the contrary, many grapes need to have their weaknesses balanced by complementary varieties.

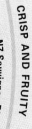

OAKY AND FRUITY

OAKY

FRUITY

Grand Cru Burgundy

top Californian, Australian, NZ, South African and Italian Chardonnay

good Burgundy

oaked Rioja

Graves and Pessac-Léognan

Australian oaked Semillon

Australian Chardonnay/Semillon

mid-priced Chardonnay from Australia, California, Washington and Chile

top NZ and South African Riesling

Alsace Pinot Gris

Australian and NZ Semillon/Sauvignon

oaked South African Chenin Blanc

cool-climate Chardonnay from the USA, Canada and NZ

mid-priced Chardonnay from South Africa and southern France

Hungarian Chardonnay

Viognier from southern France

NZ Sauvignon Blanc (South Island)

AROMATIC AND OAKY

Viognier from the northern Rhône (Condrieu and Château-Grillet)

Viognier from Australia and California

NZ Sauvignon Blanc (North Island)

good Rhône whites from Marsanne and Roussanne

Californian Fumé Blanc

Bulgarian Chardonnay

vin de pays Sauvignon Blanc

Colombard

simple vins de pays

Australian Chenin Blanc and Verdelho

Chilean Sauvignon Blanc

South African Sauvignon Blanc

CRISP AND FRUITY

top NZ Sauvignon Blanc

SIMPLE

LIGHT AND SIMPLE

LIGHT AND SIMPLE

LIGHT AND

Müller-Thurgau

Liebfraumilch

Trebbiano

Soave

Muscadet

Verdicchio

Orvieto

Vinho Verde

Alsace Pinot Blanc

Oregon Pinot Gris

cheap South African Chenin Blanc

Entre-Deux-Mers and Bordeaux Blanc

North Italian Chardonnay

NE Italian Pinot Grigio and basic Pinot Bianco

unoaked Chablis and basic Burgundy

Austrian Grüner Veltliner

dry German Riesling (Rhine)

Washington Riesling

Austrian Riesling

Vouvray and Saumur

Sancerre and Pouilly-Fumé

Australian Riesling

Rueda

unoaked white Rioja

Premier and Grand Cru Chablis (unoaked)

CRISP

AROMATIC

Alsace Gewürztraminer

Gewürztraminer from Australia, NZ and Chile

off-dry German Riesling (Rhine)

Alsace Muscat

Argentine Torrontés

Italian and southern French dry Muscat

Hungarian Gewürztraminer

Alto Adige Gewürztraminer

Rías Baixas

off-dry German Riesling (Mosel)

New York Riesling

Alsace Riesling

off-dry German Riesling (Mosel)

dry German Riesling (Mosel)

CRISP AND AROMATIC

White wine wheel

This wheel of dry white wine styles works in the same way as the red wine wheel on pages 12–13. The wines at the outer edge have layers of intense flavour; those near the centre are light and simple.

Fruity Peachy, tropical fruit or honeyish flavours without the buttery overlay of oak.

Crisp Fresh, clean flavours with a bite, like lime, gooseberry or green apples.

Aromatic Wines with intense floral or exotic fragrances such as lychees and rose petals.

Oaky Wines with the toasty, buttery flavours that come from oak barrels.

Wine flavours

Increasing intensity

KEY
The styles I have described in this chapter fit the zones of the wheel like this:

Bone dry, neutral whites The lightest wines in the CRISP zone.

Green, tangy whites CRISP wines, but shading into FRUITY and into AROMATIC styles.

Intense, nutty whites These are OAKY wines; the best are intense but subtle.

Ripe, toasty whites Wines full of OAKY and FRUITY flavours.

Aromatics They have the AROMATIC zone to themselves, but some are OAKY too.

10. Ripe, toasty whites

Upfront flavours of peaches, apricots and tropical fruits, spiced up by the vanilla, toast and butterscotch richness of new oak barrels: delicious, instantly lovable and utterly moreish.

This is what most people mean when they talk about Chardonnay today. It's the flavour that spearheaded the revolution in winemaking and wine-drinking around the world. The style was virtually invented in Australia, but it's also the hallmark of most Chardonnay in the USA and South America. Chardonnay from Penedès in Spain and many Italian versions also fit in here. Not that the style is confined to Chardonnay. It's not so difficult to give lots of different whites that tropical flavour, and new oak barrels will supply the toast and butterscotch.

11. Aromatics

Perfumy white wines combining exotic fragrances with aromas of spring flowers.

It seems impossible that a wine could smell and taste the way Gewurztraminer from Alsace does. It's packed solid with roses and lychees, face cream and a whole spice cupboard. No, it's not subtle, but with spicy food, especially Chinese, it can be wonderful.

Nowhere else in the world has the nerve to produce such over-the-top Gewurztraminer. German versions are more floral, and the Italians do their best to make their Traminer as toned-down as possible.

If you want this sort of full-blown aroma on other grapes, then it's back to Alsace. Dry Muscat here is floral with a heady, hothouse grape scent.

You want some more aromatic grapes? Viognier, at its apricots-and-spring flowers best in the Rhône Valley, is planted in the South of France, California and Australia as well; and Albariño from north-west Spain is also apricotty, but crisper. Irsai Olivér from Hungary and Torrontés from Argentina are both heady and perfumed. Müller-Thurgau from Germany or New Zealand is reminiscent of pot-pourri: all right for a glass maybe, but you don't want too much.

12. Sparkling wines

Fizz must make you feel brighter and better – but good bubbly can have delicious flavours as well.

Champagne – the genuine article from the Champagne region of northern France – sets the standard. Good Champagne has a nutty, bready aroma, appley freshness and fine bubbles. Don't buy the cheapest, though: much of it is too acidic to be drinkable, let alone enjoyable.

Sparkling wine from Australia, California and New Zealand is made in the same way and it's often just as good and usually cheaper. Much of the best stuff is made by subsidiaries of French Champagne producers.

Other good French fizzes are the slightly honeyish Crémant de Bourgogne from Burgundy, the rather sharp sparkling Saumur from the Loire Valley and the appley Blanquette de Limoux from the South.

Italian sparklers made from Chardonnay and Pinot Noir are in the Champagne style, but light, creamy Prosecco and sweet, grapy Asti can be more fun. The best Lambrusco is snappy and refreshing, but the sweetened stuff is pretty dull. Spanish Cava can be a bit earthy, but is good value. German Riesling Sekt can be okay.

Australian sparkling *red* wines are wild things, packed with pepper and jam. You'll love them or hate them, but you haven't lived until you've given them a try.

13. Golden, sweet whites

Rich, luscious mouthfuls for dessert time or when you're in a contemplative mood, often with intense flavours of peach, apricot and honey.

In France the sweet wines of Bordeaux are at their gorgeous best in Sauternes and Barsac. These are rich and syrupy wines with intense flavours of peaches and pineapples, barley sugar, butterscotch and honey, all balanced by acidity. Monbazillac, Cérons, Loupiac and Ste-Croix-du-Mont are happy hunting grounds for cheaper, lighter versions. California and Australia have a few intensely rich wines in this style, too.

The Loire Valley produces rather unusual sweet wines that are less rich and often less expensive. They're quince-flavoured with a firm acid grip and a minerally streak. Quarts de Chaume, Bonnezeaux and Vouvray are the wines to look for. Only a few Vouvrays are sweet; they're labelled as *moelleux* or *liquoreux*.

Alsace sweeties are rich and unctuous enough to partner foie gras, and that takes some doing. Sélection de Grains Nobles is sweeter than Vendange Tardive, and Gewurztraminer versions will be fatter than Pinot Gris, which will in turn be fatter than Riesling.

The sweet wines of Germany have a language all of their own. Beerenauslese and Trockenbeerenauslese are intensely sweet and extremely expensive; Auslese is less sweet and less expensive. All should be very high quality, and the best are made from Riesling: its piercing acidity keeps the sweetness from being overpowering. Austria's sweet wines are similar in style to Germany's, but weightier.

There's also a rarity called Eiswein made from frozen grapes picked in the depths of winter which manages a thrilling marriage of fierce acidity and unctuous sweetness. Apricotty Canadian icewine is made in the same way.

Hungary's Tokaji has a wonderful sweet-sour smoky flavour and quality is very high. Simple sweet Muscat from Spain, such as Moscatel de Valencia, is fairly basic but incredibly good value.

TWO TYPES OF SWEETNESS

Sweet wine is wine that is perceptibly sugary – you can detect the sweetness on your tongue tip. However, an ever-increasing number of modern dry wines emphasise ripe fruit flavours, which I often describe as **sweet fruits** to do them justice. Fruit is at its most delicious when it's ripe, and it's sheer joy to taste those flavours in a wine.

14. Warming, fortified wines

Sweet wines tasting of raisins and brown sugar, often densely packed with other flavours.

Port, the rich red fortified wine of Portugal's Douro Valley, is the classic dark sweet wine and no imitator can match the power or the finesse of the best. Australia and South Africa both make interesting port-style wines. The Portuguese island of Madeira produces some of the most exciting warming fortifieds, with rich brown smoky flavours and a startling acid bite: Bual and Malmsey are the sweet ones to look out for.

Oloroso dulce is a rare and delicious sherry with stunning concentrated flavours. Cheap sweetened 'brown' sherry is a weak parody of this style. Australian sweet Muscat from the Rutherglen region is rich and dark, even treacly. From the islands off southern Italy, the fortified Marsala of Sicily and Moscato di Pantelleria are good brown-sugar drinks with a refreshing sliver of acidity.

15. Tangy, fortified wines

Bone dry wines with startling stark, sour and nutty flavours. It's a taste that takes a bit of getting used to but which is well worth acquiring.

These are the original sherries from Jerez in southern Spain, not the dull, sweetened drinks that are exported in bulk. *Fino* is pale in colour, very dry with a thrilling tang. *Manzanilla* can seem even drier, even leaner, and has a wonderful sourdough perfume and tingling acidity. *Amontillado* is dark and nutty. Traditional *amontillado* is dry, not medium-sweet as we often see it. Dry *oloroso* adds deep, burnt flavours and at best is one of the world's greatest wines.

Montilla-Moriles is the neighbouring region to Jerez and produces similar wines, but these rarely reach the standard of good sherry. The driest style of Madeira, Sercial, is tangy, steely and savoury; Verdelho is a bit fuller and fatter. Australia and South Africa make excellent sherry-style wines, though without the tang of top-class Spanish *fino* or *manzanilla*.

What makes each wine unique

IT DOESN'T TAKE MUCH to make wine. In fact, a grape is quite capable of doing it by itself. The moment the skin of a ripe grape splits, the sugary juice on the inside comes into contact with yeasts that live naturally in the air and on the surface of the grape skin. Yeasts have a voracious appetite for sugar and as they eat their way through it they convert it into alcohol. The process is called fermentation.

But leaving nature to make wine for you like this is a bit like leaving your car out in the rain to get washed: the results will not be entirely what you were hoping for. Some 500 chemical compounds have been identified in wine, and most are produced naturally during fermentation. The job of a good winemaker is to ensure that the right compounds – the ones that taste good – are formed, and that the wrong ones – the ones that taste of rancid butter, or vinegar – are not.

Given 500 different components, it's not surprising that no two wines taste quite alike. But the winemaking process is only part of the story. The grape variety, the yield from the vine, the climate and the location of the vineyard all contribute crucially to the flavour of the wine.

Grapes and yields

Just as different varieties of apples have quite different tastes and textures, every variety of grape makes wine with its own hallmark flavours. The majority of the world's wines are produced from one or more of the 15 or 20 most popular grape varieties.

How many grapes each vine produces affects both the flavour of the wine and the price. Higher yields mean lower prices – that's obvious. But do low yields mean higher quality? To a large extent, yes. A Pinot Noir vineyard in Burgundy where the vines are pruned hard every winter to prevent the vine producing too many bunches will make better wine, other things being equal, than one where the vines are allowed to crop too heavily. More grapes, in this instance, mean more dilute juice and less flavour.

But the equation is not always a straightforward one. Each vineyard, and each grape variety, has its own optimum yield. To allow the vines to produce more than that level means a drop in quality, but the same optimum yield doesn't apply to every vineyard.

I'll give you an example. The warmer parts of Australia have heavily irrigated vineyards churning out wine like milch cows, and it's amazingly cheap. Clever winemaking and vine-growing techniques mean that it tastes pretty good, too. On the other side of the coin are the lovingly tended, 100-year-old vines boasted by other parts of Australia: these gnarled centenarians give tiny quantities of intense, concentrated, high quality wines that cost a

---

 Wine terms | Winemakers

The winemaking process, or **vinification**, is the point at which the natural events of fermentation are shaped and controlled with a view to creating a particular end product. The person who makes the decisions is the **winemaker**. The concept of the winemaker as an interventionist who determines the character of the wine is a modern one, developed in California and Australia in the 1970s. Previously it was an unsung role. An attentive winemaker can make decent wine even from unexceptional grapes and a talented one can produce stunning wine from top quality raw materials. A poor winemaker, on the other hand, can turn out dreadful wine even as neighbouring producers are creating classics. For this reason the name of the **producer**, the company that produces the wine, is a better guide to a wine's quality than the grape or the region.

Kim Milne is an Australian 'flying winemaker' – making fresh, fruity wines for producers around the world.

🍷 Wine terms | **Terroir**

This French term is at the root of the French attitude to wine. The **terroir** of each vineyard is what makes it unique: it can be defined as a combination of soil, climate and exposure to the sun. It thus sums up every possible factor: the type of topsoil and subsoil, the direction of the wind, the degree of shelter from frost, whether the ground slopes and how much, and whether it faces north, south, east or west. New World winemakers are more inclined to focus on **climate** as being the main determinant of wine style, but many are beginning to think that the concept of terroir does have some value.

bomb. Their yield is perhaps one-twentieth of that of the irrigated vineyards. But if you treated those factory-farmed vineyards the same way as the centenarian ones, you still wouldn't get the quality of the latter. And yet the wine would cost nearly as much to produce.

Climate and location

Vines are remarkably adaptable plants, and within certain limits (not too baking hot, not too freezing cold) will grow wherever you stick them in the ground. But traditional wisdom asserts that great wines are produced only at the 'margin'. What does it mean? Well, we're talking about climate. It means that the most complex wines, the ones with most finesse, most depth, most ability to evolve with age, are produced where the grapes will only just reach the required level of ripeness.

When it comes to traditional wines, like France's Chablis, Bordeaux and Burgundy, Germany's Riesling or Italy's Barolo, I have to agree with the traditional view. But there are also many modern classics from California, Australia, Chile, Argentina and South Africa, where grapes ripen fully every year without much effort at all.

Even so, a balance between heat and cool is important, and every grape variety requires different conditions to ripen. Riesling can ripen perfectly in the cool valleys of Germany; Syrah can't. But Riesling would bake in the Rhône Valley, where Syrah gaily broils to perfect ripeness under the sun's bright glare.

And the wine style matters too. If you're after delicacy, perfume, appetising balance and relatively low alcohol,

Location plays a major role in determining the style of a wine. (CLOCKWISE FROM TOP LEFT) 1. *Irrigation is the key to producing simple bulk wines in hot regions such as California's Central Valley; it's widely practised in the New World but at present is illegal in much of Europe.* 2. *The unirrigated terraces of the Douro Valley in Portugal produce smaller quantities of grapes with more intense flavours.* 3. *Early morning mists help make the Yarra Valley one of the coolest regions of Australia – ideal for sparkling wines.* 4. *Large stones gather heat during the day and radiate it at night, a recipe for rich, ripe wines from Châteauneuf-du-Pape in the South of France.*

essentials

VINTAGE WINE

It's a phrase you often hear bandied about to suggest high living: drinking vintage wine, it is implied, is far, far smarter than drinking mere wine. Well, I've got news for you. Most wine is vintage wine.

Vintage wine is simply wine from a single year: the vintage is the name for the annual grape harvest. It does not carry any connotations of greater age or distinction, like vintage cars. If a bottle has a year on it that tells you when it was made, then it's vintage wine.

Not all wine is vintage wine, and not all is the worse for it. For example, most Champagne and other good sparkling wines are non-vintage, meaning that they're a blend of wines from two or more years. Blending different years here ensures consistency of flavour and style.

you want your vines to creep to ripeness through a long, not too hot summer and autumn – marginal conditions in other words. But if you're after a great big beast of a wine with a hefty wallop of ultra-ripe fruit, well to hell with all this margin business – get that sunshine switched on to full.

And don't forget the soil. Waterlogged soil is cold and hinders ripening; well-drained soils promote it. Hillsides drain well and, if they're facing in the right direction, catch more sun; valley floors drain less well and often cop a snap of frost too. And these conditions can lie right next to each other, in the same village. They'll produce totally different wines.

And all this means…

Ideally, it all means perfect grapes. Or as good as the grower can get them: picked at optimum ripeness, with an optimum balance of sugar and acidity. Grapes like this, delivered in perfect health (no rot, no mildew) are at the absolute peak of their potential. Whether the wine lives up to that potential depends entirely on the skill and attentiveness of the winemaker.

Expert tips

Finding out about vintages

Some of the world's most sought-after wines come from places where the grapes are poised on a knife-edge of ripening or failing every year. These are the regions where vintages really matter, because the wines can be so different from one year to the next. In regions with a more reliable climate, the vintage year on the bottle is really no more than an indication of the wine's age.

You'll find vintage charts, giving a mark out of ten to each vintage in the world's main wine regions, in many places – you may even have one in your diary. How closely should you follow them?

The answer is that such general information can only ever be a rough guide. Weather conditions are not necessarily the same for a whole region, and in any case a good producer will make better wine in a poor year than a lazy one will make in a good year. So consult vintage charts for general advice – but don't treat them as gospel.

Age and maturity

As wine lies in its bottle, it evolves. Tannins soften, acid mellows, red wines grow paler and develop sediment, whites darken to a rich, nutty amber. Wines with plenty of acid and tannin will become more approachable and less fierce-tasting with time, and if they have the vital extra ingredient – loads of intense fruit flavour – the true quality of the wine will be revealed only after a few years in the bottle.

But older wine is not always better wine. For most wine the best vintage is the most recent one. Everyday wines simply taste more and more stale, faded and dull as the aging process goes on.

Making wine

So much for the background; what about the sticky business of transforming fresh-picked grapes into the world's most delicious and intriguing drink? You won't see many jolly peasants treading the grapes these days; think, rather, of stainless steel, computers and laboratory-style hygiene. Constant experimentation with equipment and techniques is part and parcel of the modern wine industry, but for all that winemaking remains a magical, messy process.

The first thing you need to do is get at the juice. A little controlled violence has to be applied in the form of a machine called a crusher which breaks the skins of the grapes. If you are making white wine, the next job after crushing is to get the fermenting juice (known as the must) well away from all the skins and stems. They add tannin and colour to the wine – exactly what you don't want for a white wine. So you transfer the crushed mass to a press without delay and squeeze out all the liquid, then pump it into a container called a vat to ferment. Some winemakers put uncrushed bunches of grapes straight into the press to get even fresher juice.

The single greatest advance in winemaking in the 20th century was the advent of temperature-controlled fermentation – for which read cool fermentation. Cool fermentation is one of the reasons why the least expensive Australian or Chilean wine, grown in conditions that are too hot for comfort, still tastes fresh and fruity. Most modern easy-drinking whites are made in great big refrigerated steel vats, but some top dry whites will be fermented in small oak barrels, which add buttery, vanilla richness to the wine.

You make red wine by fermenting the juice and the skins together, since the skins contain the colour as well as flavours, perfumes and the preservative tannin. This is generally done in a vat made of stainless steel, concrete or sometimes wood. Let the temperature go much higher than for whites to extract as much colour and flavour from the skins as possible. You'll have to stir the vat or pump the juice from the bottom over the skins floating on top, but otherwise just sit back and watch the deep purple colour ooze out of the skins. When you have as much colour and tannin as you want, drain the free-running juice into a fresh container and put the remaining pulp into a press to squeeze out the rest.

For rosé wine, start as if you were about to make red wine, but separate the must from the skins much earlier, so that the wine has just a tinge of colour. Then proceed as if you were making white wine. You can cheat by mixing a bit of red wine into a white wine, but that's not real rosé and it won't taste as good.

After fermentation

Fermentation is complete when all the sugar in the wine has turned to alcohol, or the alcohol level becomes high enough to kill the yeasts. Next the winemaker has the opportunity to transform the wine by blending the contents of two or more vats together. That could mean putting together different grape varieties to add a whole new dimension of flavour.

The wine is not ready to bottle yet: you need to mature it for anything from a few days to several years, depending on the flavour you are aiming at. Storing the wine in small oak barrels called barriques adds rich, toasty

OPPOSITE *A press separates the skins, pips and stems from the grape must. For white wines the grapes are pressed before fermentation begins; red wines are pressed at the end of the process.* ABOVE *To extract colour from the skins of red grapes, fermenting must is pumped over the cap of skins and froth that forms in the vat.*

flavours. The newer the barrels, the greater their influence on the flavour. Oak-aging doesn't automatically make a wine better – it suits gutsy wines like Cabernet Sauvignon, but would overpower a delicate Riesling.

Barrels are expensive and an economical alternative is to add oak chips or even oak flavouring to a vat of wine. It's not subtle, it's not elegant, but it's effective for low-priced wines. Stainless steel or concrete tanks, on the other hand, give full rein to the fruit flavours of the wine and are ideal for fresh-tasting wines such as tangy Sauvignon Blanc or incisive Riesling.

While they are maturing, red wines benefit from a naturally occurring process called malolactic fermentation. A strain of bacteria converts the acid in the wine from harsh malic acid (the acid of unripe apples) to softer lactic acid, which is the main acid of milk. This isn't appropriate for some white wines, in which case the bacteria are filtered out or killed off.

Making sparkling wine

All the very best sparkling wine is made by the method developed in Champagne in France. Any sparkling wine that is labelled 'traditional method' is made in this way.

Before you begin you need to make some still wine, called the base wine, which is unbearably acidic but has the potential to make great fizz. The next step is to create the bubbles. Put the still wine into strong bottles with a little yeast and sugar to start a second fermentation. Seal them with strong stoppers, because one of the side effects of fermentation is the production of carbon dioxide gas, which builds up a lot of pressure in a sealed container. But since it cannot escape, the carbon dioxide dissolves into the wine, impatiently waiting for the day it will be released as jubilant foam and elegant trails of tiny bubbles.

Unfortunately the dead yeast leaves a decidedly uncelebratory deposit of gunge in the bottle. To get this out you first have to tip it all towards the opening. In the cellars of Champagne houses, thousands of bottles are stored in angled racks where they are turned and gently tapped every day for anything up to three months to achieve this.

Once all this sediment is in the neck of the bottle, you freeze the neck and whip out the stopper: the sediment will shoot out like a pellet. Add a little sweetening to take the harsh edge off the acidity and push in the famous super-strong Champagne cork – all without losing that valuable carbon dioxide gas.

Other methods for producing sparkling wine share the same objective: to dissolve carbon dioxide into the wine and preserve the bubbles in the bottle. The tank (or Charmat) method employs a large sealed tank which works in the same way as a giant bottle. The transfer method starts off in bottles as for Champagne, but then swaps to a tank for filtering. The cheapest, and worst, option is to pump still wine full of carbon dioxide in the same way as you would a fizzy drink. You'll get large bubbles that disappear almost as soon as you have opened the bottle, and some very disappointed and dyspeptic friends.

Making sweet wine

For wine to be sweet, there must be a noticeable amount of sugar left in it after fermentation. This is known as residual sugar. The simplest method is to stop the fermentation before all the sugar has been turned into alcohol – all you need is a centrifuge or a filter. This is the cheapest way, for the cheapest wines.

Good sweet wines need grapes that are so ripe that the yeasts cannot ferment all the sugar before the alcohol level kills them off. Intense sweet wines – notably Sauternes from Bordeaux in France – come from grapes affected by a fungus called **noble rot** or, more properly, **botrytis**. It's 'noble' because rather than ruining the grapes like any other disease would, it reduces their water content and concentrates the sugar and acidity.

An Italian technique is to leave the grapes to shrivel for several months after picking before making the wine. The wines are called *passito* or *recioto*.

Making fortified wine

Sweet or dry wines with 15 per cent alcohol or more are usually made by adding brandy or pure spirit to the wine. The practice of fortifying certain wines with extra alcohol developed in order to help them travel well.

Take port: two or three hundred years ago nobody much liked the then rough red wines of the Douro Valley. Adding brandy to the fermenting wine to stop the fermentation (yeasts can't live if the alcohol level rises too high) made them both alcoholic and deliciously sweet – and that's how they've stayed.

Sherry is different: here the brandy is added after the fermentation has finished, so the wine is dry. In barrel, fino sherry grows a layer of yeast called flor, which gives it its typical pungent, almost sour flavour. Sweet sherry is sweetened before bottling.

OPPOSITE *Champagne bottles are stored head-down in racks called pupitres to collect the sediment.* THIS PAGE (CLOCKWISE FROM TOP LEFT) *1. Sweet Hungarian Tokaji develops a rich colour as it ages. 2. Grapes withered by botrytis look ugly but make delicious sweet wine. 3. Flor grows on the surface of sherry to give it a unique tangy flavour.*

Discover grape varieties

THE SIMPLEST WAY to get to know your way around wine flavours is through grape variety. As I said earlier, each grape variety has its own hallmark flavours, so two wines with different names made in places thousands of miles apart will have a fair amount in common if they're made from the same variety.

Not all wines are made from a single grape variety. Red Bordeaux, for example, usually contains at least three, and one of Australia's classic wine styles is a blend of two famous varieties: Cabernet Sauvignon and Shiraz. But once you know the taste of different grapes you'll have a good idea of what to expect from a blend.

Red wine grapes

I'm going to start with the red grapes – some people call them black, but they're deep purple or bluish in reality, so I reckon it's easier to link them to the type of wine they generally make. There's more to red wine than sturdiness, power and 'good with red meats and cheese'. Delicacy, freshness and intriguing perfumes are all within the scope of the world's red grape varieties.

Barbera

This is a high-quality, characterful grape, yet without a single world-famous wine style to its name. Its base is in north-west Italy, in Piedmont, where it makes wines so Italian-tasting that you find yourself instantly craving a plate of pasta. It's that herby, sour-cherries bite that does it: Barbera is the epitome of the mouthwatering, sweet-sour style I talked about earlier. It's sharp, rasping and acidic, but it's low in gum-puckering tannin.

It appears in umpteen guises all over Piedmont, but Barbera d'Alba and Barbera d'Asti are the best versions to go for. California uses Barbera for its simplest wines, but there's good stuff from Argentina. ***Not to be confused with*** *Barbaresco, a tough, tannic wine from the same region of north-west Italy.*

Cabernet Sauvignon
See panel, opposite.

Gamay

Gamay, to all intents and purposes, equals Beaujolais. It's one of those freaks of wine that this grape happens to flourish on an expanse of granite hills in the south of Burgundy, and effectively nowhere else. The Ardèche region of southern France has some, as does the Loire Valley in the west. But that's about it.

Gamay is never a grape to take too seriously. It makes refreshing light wines with sharp, candy-like cherry and raspberry flavours, perfect for drinking lightly chilled on

---

 Wine terms | **Noble Grapes**

Some grapes have achieved such a level of greatness in a particular region that they have been elevated to the peerage of the grape world and are often referred to as noble grapes. The major examples are: **Cabernet Sauvignon** in Bordeaux, France; **Chardonnay** and **Pinot Noir** in Burgundy, France; **Syrah** in France's Rhône Valley and in South Australia, where it's called **Shiraz**; **Chenin Blanc** and **Sauvignon Blanc** in France's Loire Valley; **Nebbiolo** in Piedmont, Italy; **Sangiovese** in Tuscany, Italy; **Riesling** in Germany; and **Zinfandel** in California.

Zinfandel is California's contribution to the nobility.

1992

A. RAFANELLI
ZINFANDEL
DRY CREEK VALLEY
SONOMA COUNTY
UNFILTERED
PRODUCED AND BOTTLED BY
A. RAFANELLI WINERY
HEALDSBURG, CALIFORNIA
Alcohol 14.1% by volume

Cabernet Sauvignon

The epitome of the intense, blackcurranty style of red wine, Cabernet Sauvignon is never among the lightest of reds – though it can be tremendously elegant. The best mature slowly to balance sweet blackcurrant flavours with a scent of cedar, cigar boxes and lead pencil shavings. It is often blended with Merlot for a richer flavour.

Where it grows Almost every country where wine is made has a fair bit of Cabernet in its vineyards. Bordeaux is its homeland, but you'll find it in the South of France as well. Italy has some top class versions; good Spanish ones come mostly from Navarra or Penedès; and it produces inexpensive wine over large tracts of Eastern Europe, notably in Bulgaria.

New World examples are vibrantly fruity, with rich, soft tannins and sometimes a touch of mint or eucalyptus. California and Australia have world-class examples; Chile is excellent value at the less expensive end; and South Africa is getting better and better. New Zealand goes for a style more like that of Bordeaux.

Keep it or drink it? Lots of people think of Cabernet Sauvignon as being a wine that needs to age in bottle after you buy it, but that's only because the best red Bordeaux and top California and Australian Cabernets need age. Most New World Cabernets, and most less expensive red Bordeaux, can be drunk straight away.

Buff's choice The top Bordeaux châteaux Lafite-Rothschild, Latour, Haut-Brion, Mouton-Rothschild and Margaux are legendary.

Best value Bulgaria, Chile and southern France are the places for tasty bargains.

Cabernet with food Modern Cabernet is an all-purpose red, but it's best with plain-cooked red meats.

Not to be confused with Cabernet Franc, a related variety, or the white grape Sauvignon Blanc.

The thick skins of Cabernet Sauvignon grapes are packed with tannin, which can make wine taste tough if the fruit is underripe.

hot summer days. A good Beaujolais-Villages is your best bet: the simplest Beaujolais and Beaujolais Nouveau often lack fruit flavour.

The ten top villages in Beaujolais, called the Beaujolais *crus*, make slightly more serious wines, some of which can mature for a few years. But Gamay is almost always a grape to drink young.

Grenache

Some like it hot, and Grenache just loves the roasting vineyards of Spain and the South of France. It pumps out ultra-ripe fruit that makes wines high in alcohol with sweet and peppery flavours, but it does best in blends: add a tougher, more aggressive partner like Syrah/Shiraz and you've got full, warm, hearty wine with sweet-natured fruit and spice. That said, if you ever come across a heady,

ORGANIC WINES

There is a strong move in grape growing, as in many other crops, towards organic methods of cultivation. All over the world there are growers who are eschewing chemical pesticides, herbicides and fertilisers, and returning to natural methods. There are no international standards for what constitutes organic viticulture, but there are local organisations in many regions.

However, vines face tough problems in most parts of the world. Fungal diseases like downy mildew and powdery mildew can wipe out a crop, and insect pests can spread deadly viruses or themselves weaken vines. The risk of abandoning chemicals altogether can be just too great. So a popular alternative to full organic viticulture is to reduce the use of chemicals to the bare essentials.

Biodynamics goes to the other extreme, taking the concept of working with rather than against nature a stage further than full organic viticulture. Vineyard practices are timed to gain maximum benefit from natural rhythms, even including the phases of the moon and the movement of the planets.

juicy rosé, there's a good chance that it's made from one hundred per cent Grenache.

It's actually a Spanish grape, and its original name is Garnacha Tinta. It beefs up the blend of some red Riojas, makes Rioja and Navarra *rosado* (the Spanish for rosé) in increasingly good light styles and produces extremely concentrated, often expensive, rich, full-bodied reds in Priorat. The concentrated style is also made in Australia: look in particular for Grenache from old vines. California and Washington State make lighter examples.

But Grenache is, as I said, at its best in good company, and it finds it in France, in the southern Rhône Valley. Grenache features among no fewer than 13 permitted grape varieties in this region's most famous wine, Châteauneuf-du-Pape – a complex, sweet-scented red with a peppery finish. The raspberry/strawberry character of this grape shines alongside a hint of hot, dusty earth in the softest Côtes du Rhône and Côtes du Rhône-Villages. Vin de pays Grenache from the neighbouring Ardèche region is light, fruity and good value.

Also known as *Garnacha or Garnacha Tinta in Spain.*

Merlot
See panel, opposite.

Nebbiolo

If you taste it too young, Nebbiolo could well be the most fiercely aggressive red you will ever encounter. It takes a few years for the staggering levels of tannin and acid to relax their grip and release the remarkable flavours of tar and roses, backed up by chocolate, cherries, raisins and prunes, and an austere perfume of tobacco and herbs. It's the severest incarnation of the sweet-sour style of Italian reds, always at its best with sturdy food.

Nebbiolo is virtually exclusive to the Piedmont region of north-west Italy. The classic wines are the forbidding Nebbiolos from Barolo and Barbaresco. Modern styles mature in five years rather than the traditional 20, which is a relief for modern wine drinkers. Softer, plummier

Merlot

Juicy, fruity wine that is lower in tannic bitterness and higher in alcohol than Cabernet Sauvignon, with which it is often blended. Blackcurrant, black cherry and mint are the hallmark flavours.

Where it grows Merlot started out as Cabernet Sauvignon's support act in Bordeaux, but has risen to worldwide popularity. The great wines of Pomerol and St-Émilion in Bordeaux are based on Merlot, with Cabernet in the blend. These wines show Merlot at its toughest and most intense, but they're still fruitier and juicier than Bordeaux's top Cabernet-based wines.

Chile is Merlot heaven, at best producing gorgeous garnet-red wines of unbelievably crunchy fruit richness that just beg to be drunk. California and Washington State have more serious aspirations for the grape, but the soft, juicy quality still shines through. Australia and South Africa are only just catching on, but Merlot already makes some of New Zealand's best reds.

Italy uses Merlot to produce a light quaffing wine in the Veneto region, though offers more flavoursome examples from Friuli, Alto Adige and Tuscany. Hungary and Bulgaria are making rapid progress with the grape. In the hot South of France Merlot tends to lack distinctive character.

Keep it or drink it? In general, drink it young, especially Chilean and Eastern European examples. Top Bordeaux Merlots, however, can last for up to 20 years.

Buff's choice Château Pétrus and Château le Pin from the Pomerol region of Bordeaux are the two most expensive wines in the world.

Best value When it's good, you can't beat young Merlot from Chile.

Merlot with food Merlot is a great all-rounder, but savoury foods with a hint of sweetness, such as honey-roast ham, particularly suit the soft fruitiness.

The wine from these Merlot grapes will be blended with Cabernet Sauvignon to produce a classic blackcurranty Bordeaux red.

Pinot Noir

At its best Pinot Noir is hauntingly beautiful with a seductive silky texture; at worst it is heavy or insipid. Good young Pinot has a sweet summer-fruit fragrance and taste. The best mature to achieve unlikely and complex aromas of truffles, game and decaying leaves.

Where it grows Pretty widely these days, since winemakers tend to fall in love with it and want it for their own. Its home is in Burgundy, and the aim of all those acolytes worldwide is to make a wine that tastes like great red Burgundies such as Volnay or Vosne-Romanée. A lot would be happy to make something that tastes like decent Bourgogne Rouge. It's probably the least obliging of all the internationally grown vines, and obstinately refuses to taste as it should unless you treat it precisely as it likes. However, the best examples from California, Oregon and New Zealand show that winemakers there have cracked it. Versions from elsewhere can be less convincing.

Keep it or drink it? Drink it, on the whole. Only the best examples repay keeping – and then not for as long as you'd keep the equivalent quality of Cabernet Sauvignon.

Buff's choice Grand Cru Burgundies from single vineyards in the Côte d'Or represent the pinnacle of Pinot. La Romanée-Conti is reputed to be the most valuable agricultural land in the world.

Best value Chile makes some reasonably priced examples. For a taste of true Burgundy, try a basic Bourgogne Rouge from a leading Burgundy producer.

Pinot with food This is food-friendly wine. It suits both plain and complex meat dishes. It also goes well with substantial fish, such as salmon or tuna.

Also known as Spätburgunder in Germany, Pinot Nero in Italy, Blauburgunder in Austria.

Not to be confused with The white grapes Pinot Blanc and Pinot Gris, or the related red grape Pinot Meunier.

The village of Gevrey-Chambertin produces some of the best Pinot Noir in Burgundy.

wines come from elsewhere in Piedmont – Nebbiolo d'Alba, Langhe, Gattinara, Ghemme and Carema – or under the guise of Spanna, its alternative name.

A few committed Italophiles in California are pretty much the only other producers, though a few Australians are starting to look at it seriously.
Also known as *Spanna.*

Pinot Noir
See panel, opposite.

essenziale
WHITE WINE FROM RED GRAPES

The juice inside a grape is clear, whatever the colour of the skin. So if you separate the juice from the skins before fermentation, hey presto, you'll end up with white wine.

The French call this style Blanc de Noirs and it works well with Pinot Noir in Champagne. A less edifying example of the white-from-red conjuring act is white or 'blush' Zinfandel. The problem is that you lose all the berry-fruit character that makes Zinfandel exciting.

However, making white wine from black grapes is not, apart from these two examples, all that common. In Champagne the purpose of using Pinot Noir like this is to give weight and body to the blend, and in California the original purpose of white Zinfandel was to use up a grape that was temporarily out of fashion. Demand for red wine is just too high now for red grapes to be denuded of their colour without very good reason.

Bollinger's rare and expensive Blanc de Noirs Champagne is made with Pinot Noir grapes from very old vines. The popular Woodbridge blush Zinfandel is as good as this simple white-from-red style gets.

Pinotage
Conceived, bred and developed to meet the demands of the South African soil and climate, this grape produces both rough-textured damsony wines and smoother, fruity styles with flavours of plums, bananas, redcurrants and toasted marshmallows. Either way, it's a wine to love or hate. And it's not only drinkers who are divided: while some South African producers adore it, others won't touch it. Spicy, warm-hearted reds are the best wines.

Pinotage has not ventured far afield from its South African home, but that may be set to change. New Zealand has a few vines, and Chile and Australia are now experimenting with the grape.

Sangiovese
The name of the grape might not be familiar, but it's the principal variety behind Chianti, Italy's most famous red wine. It's responsible for Chianti's tea-like bitter twist and cherry-and-plum fruit. So it's one of those mouthwatering sweetsour grapes, Italian down to its toes.

And it's not just grown for Chianti. You'll find wines labelled Sangiovese in most of Italy, though not the very north, and some will be a bit dilute and thin and acidic, but a lot will be light, attractive everyday red with herby fruit and a rasping finish – just the thing with the lunchtime pasta.

In the best parts of Tuscany, however, it is taken very seriously indeed. Big, heavyweight wines like Brunello di Montalcino and Vino Nobile di Montepulciano are made entirely from Sangiovese. These are world-class wines that need aging, as do the best Chiantis, but most Sangiovese is best drunk young and fresh.

You'll find some Sangiovese in California, Australia and Argentina, as well, and they're starting to do interesting things with it; but for the moment there is nothing to equal the best Italian wines.
Also known as Brunello, Prugnolo.

Syrah/Shiraz

Intense is the word for Syrah/Shiraz wines. Intensely rich, intensely spicy, intensely sweet-fruited, or even all three at once. The most powerful begin life dark, dense and tannic but mature to combine sweet blackberry and raspberry flavours with a velvety texture.

Where it grows Mostly in France and Australia – and unusually, the two styles are running neck and neck in terms of quality. French Syrah is more smoky, herby and austere; Australian Shiraz is richer, softer, with a leathery quality.

But Australia is a big place, and styles vary across the country. Victoria Shiraz can be more peppery, Barossa Valley Shiraz leathery and chocolaty. Old Vines Shiraz, wherever it's from, can be terrifically intense.

There's some Shiraz in South Africa, a bit in Italy and even a few vines in Switzerland. California is making some good stuff but so far it's mostly blended with other varieties. Argentina is keeping its sights set on the budget market.

Keep it or drink it? All Syrah/Shiraz needs a year or two from the vintage to hit its stride. Top wines will last for ten years, and a great Hermitage might peak at 15.

Buff's choice Hermitage or Côte-Rôtie from the northern Rhône; Grange from Australia. It's no coincidence that this wine was known for years as Grange Hermitage.

Best value Gluggers from southern France or Argentina.

Syrah/Shiraz with food This is a high-octane wine that can stand up to powerful flavours. It's not just for big dinners, though: I love it with peppered salami and tangy cheese.

Why two names? It's Syrah in France; Shiraz in Australia. Other regions use either name.

Not to be confused with Petite Sirah, a grape grown in California and Mexico.

The Syrah grapes grown on the hill of Hermitage make dark, dense wines that take years to mature.

Syrah/Shiraz

See panel, opposite.

Tempranillo

Spain's maid-of-all-work crops up all over the country, producing wines of all shapes and sizes. There are grand, prestigious wines in Ribera del Duero, ageworthy reds in Rioja and young, juicy, unoaked styles in Valdepeñas, La Mancha, Somontano and many other regions. Its flavour is good but not always instantly recognisable the way that Cabernet Sauvignon or Pinot Noir is: Tempranillo's most distinctive feature is its good whack of strawberry fruit, but in the biggest, weightiest wines this tends to go plummy and blackberryish and spicy, overlaid with vanilla oak. Only the finest wines need aging – and the simplest really must be drunk young and fresh.

In northern Portugal Tempranillo is called Tinta Roriz and it is an important grape for port, the classic fortified wine, as well as appearing in reds from both Dão and Douro. Under the alias Aragonez it's responsible for some juicy numbers from Alentejo in the south.

Argentina grows it for its vivacious fruitiness and California, Oregon and the South of France are experimenting with it.

Also known as *Ready for this? Cencibel, Tinto del País, Tinto del Toro, Tinto Fino, Tinto de Madrid or Ull de Llebre in Spain; Tinta Roriz or Aragonez in Portugal. And that's the abbreviated list.*

Zinfandel

California's speciality grape can be all things to all people. The best Zinfandel and the type I'm interested in talking about is spicy, heartwarming dry red wine. Other styles range from off-white, sweetish and insipid 'blush' wines to high-intensity sweet wine. All red California Zinfandel shares a ripe-berries fruitiness, but the intensity varies dramatically from light to blockbustingly powerful.

Cheap examples are usually lightweight juicy, fruity reds. The top-quality Zinfandels are at the sturdier end of

As each year passes this gnarled old Zinfandel vine in the Russian River Valley in California pumps more intense flavours into fewer bunches of grapes.

the scale and they're expensive. Mendocino County produces strapping Zin full of blackberry fruit, spice and tannin. It's rich, ripe, dark and chunky in Napa, rounder and spicier in Sonoma and wild and wonderful from old vineyards in the Sierra Foothills. The full-throated, brawny flavours of these big Zins will wash down anything from barbecue ribs to the richest Pacific Rim cooking.

Zinfandel from regions outside the USA, which place a lower value on the grape, are an economical alternative. It's grown in one or two outposts in Australia, South Africa and Chile and not much money will buy you a sumptuous, rich, almost overripe mouthful.

It's almost certain that Zinfandel is the same variety as the southern Italian grape Primitivo, and if you're looking for good value, Primitivo gives you the most bang for your bucks. Some Primitivo is even being labelled as Zinfandel to make it seem more fashionable.

Also known as *Primitivo in Italy and it's probably the same as Croatia's Plavac Mali, too.*

White wine grapes

Green, yellow, pinkish or even brown on the vine, these are the grapes that promise refreshment. But that's not all: white wines range from the breathtakingly sharp to the most luscious and exotic flavours you will ever encounter.

Chardonnay

See panel, opposite.

Chenin Blanc

What an extraordinary flavour – a striking contrast of rich honey, guava and quince with steely, minerally flavours and whiplash acidity. Chenin can produce gum-numbing dry wines, sparkling wines, medium-sweet styles or super-sweet noble rot-affected wonders.

Chenin accounts for the white wines of the heartland of France's Loire Valley – Vouvray, Savennières, Saumur and others. It can have a problem ripening here, but after a series of warm summers in the 1990s, and with improved techniques in both vineyard and cellar, Loire Chenin is on a roll. Simpler examples have good apple and honey fruit; others, like dry Vouvray, have a streak of minerally flavour reminiscent of sunlight flashing on granite. The best sweet Loire Chenin comes from Bonnezeaux, Quarts de Chaume and Coteaux du Layon. These wines need to mature for years to attain their full richness.

Chenin is South Africa's most widely planted grape, mostly used for simple wines, but an increasing number of winemakers are trying to extract more character. New Zealand and Australia produce small amounts of good fruity Chenin. California and Argentina use it for unmemorable simple wines. So the Loire rules. Nothing can touch it for variety, style, or value.

Gewürztraminer

There's a fragrant blast of lychee and rose petals followed up by a luxurious oil-thick texture – dry or sweet, it's the most intensely aromatic wine in the world. 'Gewürz' translates as spice, although it's difficult to think of a single spice that exactly resembles Gewürztraminer. Still, if you're searching for a wine to match spicy Asian food, look no further. It's also wonderful to sip by itself.

Alsace is the place to go for Gewurztraminer (they take the accent off the 'u' here). Even the most basic wines have a swirl of aromatic spice, while great vintages can produce super-intense wines in styles from dry to richly sweet.

Other countries seem to lose their nerve with this grape, producing sensible, well-brought-up wines that you'd be perfectly happy to take home to meet your mother. New Zealand Gewürz is like this, and Italian Traminer. German Traminer gets more floral. Only Alsace has what it takes. ***Also known as Traminer.***

 Wine terms | **Old vines**

This phrase is a great selling point on labels. **Old vines** (or **vieilles vignes** on French labels) equal more concentrated flavours, equal higher prices, equal wine that is rare and desirable – that's the theory. And it's true. Old vines are something to boast of: they give more intensely flavoured wine.

A lot of growers uproot vines that are over 25, because that's the point at which their yields of grapes begin to drop. But how old is old? Eighty or 100 years? Now that's old. Australia has some vines that old; so does California. Sixty? Yes, that's old. Forty? Merely middle-aged. Thirty? To call such vines old is a slight exaggeration. The trouble is that there is no agreed definition of what constitutes old. And we need one, badly. Old vines is generally a reliable term, but it's appearing on more and more bottles.

Vines as much as 100 years old are cherished by quality-obsessed producers.

Chardonnay

The world's favourite white grape variety can make anyone fall in love with wine, because it's so generous with its easy-to-relish buttery, lemony flavours. Chardonnay has an affinity for oak-aging and styles divide into unoaked, lean, green and reserved; lightly oaked, when it can be nutty and oatmealy; and heavily oaked, which is where butteriness, tropical fruits and butterscotch come in.

Where it grows Chardonnay is everywhere. I'd be hard pushed to name a wine-producing country that doesn't grow it. It originates from the French region of Burgundy, where it produces stylish, succulent wines with a nutty richness yet bone-dry clarity. However, in the north of Burgundy is Chablis, where Chardonnay has a sharp, minerally acidity that may or may not be countered by the richness of oak, depending on the preferences of the producer.

The New World style has its origins in Australia and California: upfront, pineappley, oaky and sumptuous. New Zealand versions are either fruity or surprisingly nutty. Chilean versions are on the fruity side. South African ones are mixed in quality, but very good at their best. In Europe, New World styles come from southern France, Italy and Spain.

Keep it or drink it? Most Chardonnay is ready the moment you buy it, but top wines from France, Australia and California will improve for five years or so.

Buff's choice Of all Burgundy's mercilessly expensive Grands Crus, Le Montrachet is finest of the fine. Top Californian Chardonnays sell at much the same price.

Best value Economical Chilean or Australian.

Chardonnay with food The whole point of modern Chardonnay is that it will go pretty well with almost anything. It is wonderful with all fish, whether lightly grilled or drowned in a rich, buttery sauce. The richer the sauce, the oakier the wine can be.

The cool Bien Nacido vineyard in Santa Maria Valley is the source of some of California's very best Chardonnay.

Muscat

The only grape to make delicious wine that actually smells of the grape itself comes in a multitude of styles. Rich, sweet and fortified, floral and dry or exuberantly frothy, Muscat wines all share a seductive grapy aroma. Intensely sweet Muscats often add an orange-peel fragrance.

To start with the darkest and sweetest, Rutherglen in north-eastern Victoria, Australia, is a sticky heaven for those who crave its raisiny, perfumed fortified Muscats. Golden, sweet Muscats, again fortified, come from the South of France (from Beaumes-de-Venise, Frontignan, Rivesaltes and other villages) and have light, delicate orange-and-grape aromas with a touch of rose petals; the best have lovely elegance. Spain's Moscatel de Valencia is cheaper, clumsier, but a good mouthful all the same.

Then there's dry Muscat. Alsace is the place for this, though Australia and Portugal both have the odd one. And for those who like a spot of fizz with their Muscat, there's Italy's deliciously grapy Asti: frothy, sweet and sparkling.

Also known as Muscat Blanc à Petits Grains (its full name), Muscat de Frontignan or, in Australia, Brown Muscat. The Italians call it Moscato. The less thrilling Muscat of Alexandria (Spain's Moscatel) and Muscadelle are related grapes.

Not to be confused with Muscadet, the bone-dry white wine from the Loire Valley in France.

Pinot Gris

Intensity is a key issue with Pinot Gris. Whether you like your white wine bone dry and neutral or rich and spicy, or anything in between, the right Pinot Gris for you is out there somewhere. A hint of honey (sometimes admittedly very faint) is the linking theme that connects the grape's different incarnations.

Rich, smoky and honeyed dry whites from Alsace in France show Pinot Gris at its most pungent. The USA has

Against a backdrop of autumn gold a late harvest of ultra-ripe grapes in the French region of Alsace will produce richly sweet wines.

essentials

CLASSIC BLENDS

The modern approach of labelling wines by the name of the grape variety has led to great popularity for single-varietal wines. Cabernet Sauvignon, Merlot, Sauvignon Blanc and Chardonnay have all swept to fame on their own merits. But many of the classic flavours of France and other European wine nations are based on blends of two or more grape varieties.

Cabernet Sauvignon may be the most famous grape of red Bordeaux, but if the wines were made solely from Cabernet, most would be unbearably austere. Merlot and other grapes in the blend soften the wine and add exciting layers of flavour.

It's the same story with Bordeaux whites. Sémillon and Sauvignon Blanc are often better together than alone, and Muscadelle (a relative of Muscat) adds a heady fragrance to the sweet wines. Champagne, Rioja, Chianti and port are all (for the most part) blended wines, and a bottle of Châteauneuf-du-Pape can include the juice of as many as 13 different grape varieties.

European blends are often emulated in the newer wine-producing nations, but new partnerships have become established too. Australia, in particular, has made modern classics of Chardonnay blended with Semillon and Cabernet Sauvignon with Shiraz.

had success with lighter, crisper, spicy versions from Oregon. Eastern Europe produces outstanding dry or off-dry and spicy wines.

Germany takes the grape into sweet-wine territory and calls it Ruländer. Dry German Grauburgunders aged in oak are crisp and more exciting. Fairly neutral wines, and plenty of them, come from Italy. But really good Italian Pinot Grigio is floral and honeyed.

Also known as Pinot Grigio in Italy, Tokay-Pinot Gris in Alsace, Ruländer (sweet) or Grauburgunder (dry) in Germany, Malvoisie in Switzerland.

Not to be confused with The other Pinots: Pinot Noir, Pinot Blanc and Pinot Meunier.

Riesling

It's not a grape that everyone takes an instant liking to, Riesling, but it has undeniable finesse. Piercing acidity is the most startling and recognisable feature in styles ranging from thrillingly dry to richly sweet, with flavours that range from apple and lime zing to peaches and honey to pebbles and slate. As Riesling ages it develops an aroma akin to petrol (altogether nicer than it sounds).

Dispel any confusion lurking in your mind between Riesling and Liebfraumilch, that simple, sweetish first step in wine drinking invented in Germany which rarely contains any Riesling at all. Riesling is the grape of Germany's greatest wines. In the Mosel region it produces mostly light, floral wines with a slaty edge. Rheingau Rieslings are generally richer, fruitier and spicy. Both are surprisingly low in alcohol. They need a few years to mature before the flavours are at their best.

Just across the border into France, Alsace makes a more alcoholic dry, spicy Riesling. Australian Riesling is different again. It has an invigorating lime aroma that goes toasty with age and a good, weighty slap of alcohol.

Other countries, including New Zealand, South Africa and the United States, have some decent Riesling, but Germany, Alsace and Australia have defined the key styles.
Also known as *Johannisberger Riesling, Rhine Riesling or White Riesling – and Riesling Renano in Italy.*
Not to be confused with *Laski Rizling, Olasz Rizling, Riesling Italico or Welschriesling.*

Sauvignon Blanc

See panel, opposite.

Sémillon

Sémillon comes into its own in two key areas, Bordeaux and Australia, though it is grown elsewhere as well, and it comes in two totally different styles: dry and sweet. Sémillon is the French way to spell it; in Australia they knock the accent off the 'e'. Either way, it can produce wonderful quality.

It pops up in various parts of Australia for dry wine, but Hunter Valley Semillon is the most famous. The traditional style here is unoaked. When young, unoaked Hunter Semillon tastes neutral and light, with just a bit of lemony fruit. But unoaked Hunter Semillon should not be drunk young. It needs up to a decade in bottle – and then it will amaze you with its waxy, lanoliny, nectarine fruit.

Oaked Australian Semillon is different. Dry, toasty and lemony, it's good young but the best can age for a few years, too. Most Australian Semillon is oaked, and some is blended with Chardonnay.

In Bordeaux Sémillon is usually blended with Sauvignon Blanc, which adds a refreshing streak of sharp acidity. The best dry versions, oaked wines with flavours of cream and nectarines, come from Graves and Pessac-Léognan. They improve for several years in bottle.

Sweet wines are another story. Here Sauternes is the star: this Bordeaux appellation produces extraordinarily concentrated wines from grapes affected by noble rot, with flavours of barley sugar and peaches. This golden, sweet style is imitated, in small quantities, in California, Australia and New Zealand. The method of production means it can never be cheap; but nor is it overpriced.

Viognier

Heady, hedonistic, with a rich scent of apricots and breeze-blown spring flowers, Viognier is an aromatic dry wine so luxurious that it seems almost sweet.

It used to be confined to a few small areas of the northern Rhône Valley in France, but fashion is a powerful force. Suddenly Viognier is appearing all over the South of France – never in large quantities, to be sure, but at prices that give a taste of the grape to those of us who can't fork out the premium-plus rates for classic top-quality Condrieu and Château-Grillet from the Rhône.

California and Australia and even South America are trying their hands at it, too. Results vary, but are distinctly promising to very good. Viognier should be drunk young and fresh – the scent doesn't last forever.

Sauvignon Blanc

This is the epitome of the green, tangy style: an unrestrained wine with aromas and flavours of grass, nettles, gooseberries and asparagus.

Where it grows New Zealand, particularly in the Marlborough region, produces what has become the classic style, all pungent gooseberries and nettles.

Australia seldom matches New Zealand for lean pungency. Chile delivers lean, fairly punchy flavours from the Casablanca region. South Africa is becoming increasingly reliable for Sauvignon Blanc. Californian versions are sometimes aged in new oak, which gives a different sort of flavour – more tropical fruit salad.

The grape's European home is in France's Loire Valley. The wines are less lean and green than New Zealand versions but, at the top of the tree, often more complex. Sancerre and Pouilly-Fumé are the main wines; Menetou-Salon, Sauvignon de Touraine and Vin de Pays du Jardin de la France are similar but cheaper.

Sauvignon is also an important grape in Bordeaux, and elsewhere in Europe there are full-flavoured Sauvignons in Spain, especially in Rueda, neutral ones in the north of Italy and light ones in Austria. Eastern European versions vary, but tend to lack pungency.

Keep it or drink it? Apart from a few top wines, Sauvignon Blanc is for drinking as soon as you can get the bottle home and the cork out.

Buff's choice Cloudy Bay from New Zealand is a cult wine that sells out as soon as it hits the shops.

Best value Entre-Deux-Mers in Bordeaux is pumping out bargains with a good tangy flavour.

Sauvignon with food Sauvignon is a good match for spicy food and tomato-based dishes.

Also known as Fumé Blanc in California and Australia.

Not to be confused with Cabernet Sauvignon, the famous red grape.

Like the wines they produce, Sauvignon Blanc grapes burst with sharp, tangy flavours.

Other grape varieties

There's plenty of wine about made from these less famous varieties. Grapes marked ✪ are my tips for future stardom.

Albariño Characterful, refreshing white from Spain tasting of apricot, peach and grapefruit, which can be expensive. Also used in Vinho Verde in Portugal.

Aligoté White grape grown in Burgundy and Eastern Europe to produce simple sharp wines. Burgundy's Aligoté de Bouzeron is best.

Cabernet Franc A relative of Cabernet Sauvignon which makes earthy, blackcurranty wines. Used in red Bordeaux blends and on its own in the Loire Valley.

Carignan Widely grown red grape in southern France, used for rough everyday wines but can be deliciously spicy or sturdy. There's lots in California.

Carmenère ✪ Red grape from Chile making marvellously spicy wines.

Cinsaut Red grape used in southern French blends, also grown in South Africa. Produces light, fresh wines.

Colombard Reliable everyday white: fruity and crisp, occasionally with tropical fruits aromas. Widely grown in southern France, Australia, California and South Africa.

Corvina The major grape of Italy's Valpolicella, a cherryish and bitter-sweet red at best.

Dolcetto Vibrant, purplish-red wine from Italy, full of fruit flavour with a bitter-cherry twist. Drink it young.

Garganega The white grape used to make Italy's famous Soave, often overcropped but green-apple fresh when good.

Malbec ✪ (also known as Cot or Auxerrois) The best red grape in Argentina, making smooth, rich reds at all price levels. It's also the major grape of Cahors in South-West France, which can be juicy and plummy at best.

Malvasia Widely grown in Italy, producing fragrant dry whites, rich, apricotty sweet whites and frothing light reds. Also grown in Spain and Portugal, it's the grape of the Madeira wine Malmsey.

Marsanne A Rhône white variety, rich and scented at best, that also makes big, broad, honeyed wines in Australia's Goulburn Valley.

Melon de Bourgogne The grape of Muscadet, the Loire Valley's simplest white wine.

Mourvèdre (also known as Mataro) Red grape that gives backbone to southern Rhône wines, also grown in Australia. Can be hard and earthy, but develops smoky, leathery flavours as it ages.

Müller-Thurgau Widely planted in Germany to produce bulk quantities of soft, floral, unexceptional white wine. Much the same happens in Eastern Europe and NZ, but it can be fresh and fine in northern Italy.

Muscadelle A fragrant white grape used for sweet wines in Bordeaux and Australia.

Palomino and **Pedro Ximénez** The white grapes behind sherry and Montilla-Moriles: Palomino for dry styles, PX for sweet ones.

Pinot Blanc A light quaffer. At best it makes creamy, floral, appley wine in Alsace; good in northern Italy too.

Roussanne A white Rhône grape – a more aromatic and elegant cousin of Marsanne.

Tannat A sturdy, spicy red grape. It originates from Madiran in France, but also does well in Uruguay.

Torrontés ✪ The star white grape of Argentina, producing highly aromatic wines.

Touriga Nacional ✪ Red grape with plenty of colour, perfume and fruit used in port and modern Portuguese dry wines. Worldwide interest is growing.

Trebbiano (also known as Ugni Blanc) White grape producing the flavourless bulk wines of Italy. Better ones are good, though still neutral.

Verdelho ✪ Originally a grape for the fortified wine of Madeira, but it's producing rich, lime-flavoured dry whites in Australia.

Verdicchio The best of Italy's neutral white grapes, used in the wine of the same name.

Vermentino Light, perfumed dry white from Sardinia.

Vernaccia White grape making an Italian equivalent to sherry in Sardinia and a (sometimes) tasty golden dry white in Tuscany.

Viura The main white grape of Spain's Rioja, light and apple-fresh on its own, or richer and longer lasting in a blend with Malvasia.

Instant recall: red grapes

Barbera A snappy, refreshing Italian red
Cabernet Sauvignon The blackcurranty red par excellence
Gamay The juicy red grape of Beaujolais
Grenache Ripe strawberry and spice, often in a blend
Merlot Juicy and plummy; part of the classic red Bordeaux blend
Nebbiolo The stern and tannic dark grape from north-west Italy
Pinot Noir A capricious grape, at best making elegant, silky reds with a haunting fragrance
Pinotage A love-it-or-hate-it sturdy red from South Africa
Sangiovese The main grape of Chianti: mouthwatering, sweet-sour red fruit flavours from Italy
Syrah/Shiraz Spicy and warm-hearted; equally at home in France's Rhône Valley and Australia
Tempranillo Spanish strawberries and plums
Zinfandel California's all-purpose grape variety, best as a spicy red.

Instant recall: white grapes

Chardonnay Ripe peaches and toast: the classic international white grape
Chenin Blanc The quirky, fruity-minerally white grape from the Loire Valley.
Gewürztraminer The uniquely spicy and exotic white, at its best in Alsace
Muscat Dry and sweet wines that actually taste of grapes
Pinot Gris Neutral in Italy, rich in Alsace, always with a hint of honey
Riesling The steely aristocrat of white grapes
Sauvignon Blanc Gooseberry and nettle tang, equally at home in New Zealand and the Loire Valley
Sémillon Lemony, waxy dry whites and golden sweeties from Bordeaux and Australia
Viognier The sumptuous, apricotty white of the Rhône Valley.

ABOVE *The deliciously fruity juice of a good Beaujolais-Villages drains from the press.* LEFT *Pinot Noir and Chardonnay, the grape varieties that made the French region of Burgundy world famous.*

Part II

Enjoying Wine

Wine is part of everyday life and treating it with reverential awe won't make it taste any better. The rituals of opening, serving, tasting, buying and storing wine are mostly built on sound reasoning, but they are meaningless if they don't help you to enjoy yourself and get the best out of your wine. What you drink and how you appreciate it are your own concerns, and when you're in a shop or restaurant these decisions are yours, not the assistant's or the waiter's.

Opening the bottle

THE GENTLE CREAK, squeak and pop of a cork being pulled – that's a sound that I like a lot. It's the overture to a celebration, the moment when work stops and the evening begins. Even the most hopeless corkscrew will work most of the time, but a well-made one is less likely to wreck the cork or leave cork crumbs floating in your wine.

Choosing a corkscrew

Look for a corkscrew with a comfortable handle, an open spiral and a lever system that you like using. Corkscrews with a solid core that looks like a giant screw tend to mash up delicate corks or get stuck in tough ones. With a simple non-levered corkscrew the effort of pulling the cork can turn into a circus-strongman act.

Using a corkscrew

First tear off or cut away the metal foil or plastic seal around the top of the bottle, known as the capsule. You can buy a device called a foil cutter for this job; some corkscrews include one in the handle. Wipe the lip of the bottle if there is dirt or mould around the top of the cork.

Press the point of the corkscrew gently into the centre of the cork. Turn the corkscrew slowly and steadily and try to drive it in dead straight. If it veers wildly off-course at the first attempt, it is better to unwind it and start again than to press on and risk breaking the cork. Some corkscrews remove the cork by driving straight through it, but for others stop turning as the point emerges at the bottom of the cork and ease the cork out gently.

Opening sparkling wine

The pressure in the bottle does the work, so all you have to do is control it. If you don't, you'll get a loud pop, a rush of foam and a half-empty bottle of rapidly flattening fizz. You might injure somebody, too.

Tear off the foil to reveal the wire cage that restrains the cork. Place one thumb over the top of the cork and undo the cage. From the moment the cage is released there is an ever-present danger of the cork shooting off, so point the bottle away from people and breakables.

Grasp the cork with one hand and hold the bottle firmly with the other. Now turn the bottle slowly while twisting the cork in the opposite direction. The cork should ease out gently. Hold the bottle at an angle of 45° for a few moments to calm the initial rush of foam, then pour the first glass. A cold bottle will open with a less dramatic burst than a warm one.

Broken corks

To remove a broken cork that is still wedged into the bottle neck, drive the corkscrew in at the sharpest available angle and press the cork fragment against the side of the neck as you work it gently upwards. If you're having no luck, push the cork down into the wine. You might get bits of cork in your glass, but the wine will taste none the worse for it – just fish them out.

If a sparkling wine cork breaks in the bottle, then your only option is to resort to a corkscrew. But take the cork out very cautiously, and try to release the pressurised gas from the bottle slowly.

essentials

BOXES, CARTONS AND CANS

Wine boxes with a tap on the side are a perfectly sound idea, especially if you just want a glass or two per day. The technology is fine; the problem is that the choice is limited and the wine in the box is rarely exciting.

Cartons like the ones used to store milk are effective, but they're awkward to open and, again, the wine put into them is nothing to write home about. As for **ring-pull cans**, don't even think about it.

The **Screwpull** brand is a very simple design, which has never been bettered. It relies on the high quality open spiral for its effectiveness. This long-handled version gives you extra leverage and makes light work of even the stiffest corks, although the foil-cutting knife is a bit tricky to use.

The most irritating design is the ubiquitous **'butterfly'** – not only does it feature the sort of thick, solid-cored screw that mashes up corks, but I always find it impossible to remove the cork in one sweep of the lever arms.

The standard restaurant corkscrew is called a **waiter's friend**. It has the advantage of folding away like a penknife, but it takes a bit of practice to get the knack of using it. I keep one handy for spontaneous picnics. This one features a very effective foil cutter in the handle.

Expert tips

Don't be a cork snob

The only requirements for the seal on a bottle of wine are that it should be hygienic, airtight, long-lasting and removable. **Cork** has stood the test of time, but it is prone to infection and shrinkage. Modern alternatives lack cork's cachet, but they can give you a fresher wine.

Plastic bungs modelled on the traditional cork are now common in budget wines and are also used by a few high-quality producers. The best plastics have a soft texture. A simple **screwtop** is the other option and snobbery is all that prevents its widespread use.

Serving wine

IF YOU WANT to taste wine at its best, to enjoy all its flavours and aromas, to admire its colours and texture, choose glasses designed for the purpose and show the wine a bit of respect.

Glasses

The ideal wine glass is a fairly large tulip shape, made of fine, clear glass, with a slender stem. Anything that approximates to this description will do. When you pour the wine, fill the glass no more than halfway to allow space for the aromas. For sparkling wines choose a tall, slender glass, as it helps the bubbles to last longer.

Coloured glass obscures the colour of the wine, flared glasses dissipate the aromas rather than concentrating them, and heavy, thick glasses are, well, heavy.

Detergent residues or grease in the glass can affect the flavour of any wine and reduce the bubbliness of sparkling wine. Always rinse glasses thoroughly after washing them and allow them to air-dry or keep a lint-free cloth for drying glasses only. Ideally wash the glasses in really hot water and use no detergent at all. Store your wine glasses upright to avoid trapping stale odours.

Decanting

There are three reasons for putting wine in a decanter: one, to separate it from sediment that has formed in the bottle; two, to let the wine breathe; three, to make it look nice. You don't need a special decanter, a jug is just as good. Equally, there's no reason why you shouldn't decant the wine to aerate it and then pour it back into the bottle again for serving.

A bottle of mature red wine that contains sediment needs careful handling. Stand it upright for a day or two to let the sediment settle to the bottom. You can serve the wine straight from the bottle if you pour it carefully, but it's safer to decant it. Place a torch or a candle beside the decanter and, as you pour the wine, stand so that you can see the light shining through the neck of the bottle. Keep pouring in one steady motion and stop when you see the sediment rushing into the neck.

Breathing

Most wines do not need to be opened early in order to let the wine breathe. A few fine red wines – top-class red Bordeaux, top Italian reds, top Syrah/Shiraz and a few others – can benefit from it, but almost all inexpensive ones, and all white wines, can simply be opened and drunk. There are no set rules, however, and only experience will tell you if a wine will improve with breathing.

The reason for letting a wine breathe is that contact with oxygen in the air makes the flavours more open. But leave the wine for too long before you drink it and you

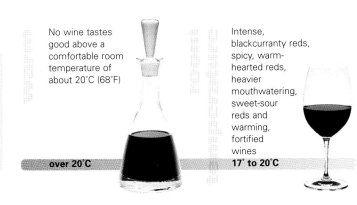

No wine tastes good above a comfortable room temperature of about 20°C (68°F)

Intense, blackcurranty reds, spicy, warm-hearted reds, heavier mouthwatering, sweet-sour reds and warming, fortified wines

over 20°C   17° to 20°C

Careful decanting is only necessary when the wine contains sediment. Stop pouring when the dark grains or sludge reach the neck of the bottle.

Expert tips

Quick tips for temperature

A fridge takes two to four hours to chill a bottle of wine, so it's not much use in an emergency. The quickest way to chill a wine is by immersing it in a bucket filled with a combination of **ice** and **cold water.** This is much faster than ice on its own. Add **salt** to the water for even quicker results. Wine chills down fairly swiftly in a freezer, too – but if you forget to take it out in time it will probably break the bottle as it freezes solid.

If a wine is too cold, the best thing is to pour the wine and then cup the glass in your hands for a minute or two. Don't use strong heat sources.

may find the flavours going flat and dull from excessive oxidation. If you're the sort of person who plans ahead, open your reds an hour or so before you intend to drink them. That way they won't suffer from oxidation, and they may even improve. And always beware of opening even top wines too early. Very old examples can lose all their flavour if they are exposed to the air for too long.

Simply uncorking the bottle and leaving it to stand will have little or no effect, as only a small surface area is exposed. Pouring off a small amount will help, but decanting will expose the wine to far more air. For instant results with a wine that has been uncorked just this minute, a quick swirl of your glass will work wonders.

Leftovers

You can keep leftover wine for several days without it losing much of its flavour. All you need to do is hold off the effects of oxidation. The simplest way is to push the cork back in and stick the bottle in the fridge. Alternatively, you can buy effective devices which suck out the air to create a partial vacuum or which inject a dense inert gas.

Special stoppers are available for recorking sparkling wine, but you can simply push in a conventional cork. Either way, keep the wine well chilled. If you have two leftover bottles of the same wine, pour the contents of both into one. The fuller the bottle the longer the wine will last. This works best with red and sparkling wines.

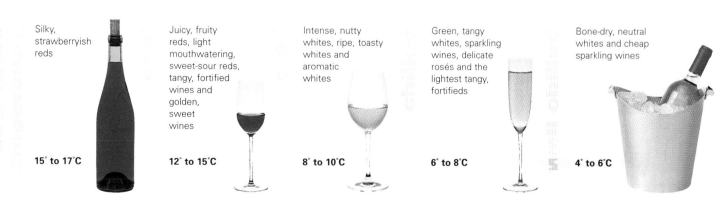

Silky, strawberryish reds

15˚ to 17˚C

Juicy, fruity reds, light mouthwatering, sweet-sour reds, tangy, fortified wines and golden, sweet wines

12˚ to 15˚C

Intense, nutty whites, ripe, toasty whites and aromatic whites

8˚ to 10˚C

Green, tangy whites, sparkling wines, delicate rosés and the lightest tangy, fortifieds

6˚ to 8˚C

Bone-dry, neutral whites and cheap sparkling wines

4˚ to 6˚C

How to taste wine

As YOU TRY MORE and more wines, your awareness of flavour and your personal preferences will develop. Most important of all, you'll be able to apply this knowledge when choosing wine in a wine shop or restaurant.

But what's so special about wine that you have to go through a whole ritual just to say what it tastes like? Well, wine doesn't just taste of wine. Any number of aromas and flavours mingle together in the glass and if you just knock it back the same way you do a cold beer or a soft drink, you could be missing most of whatever flavour the wine has to offer.

Drinking and tasting wine attentively is by far the best method for finding your way around the grapes, regions and styles of the wine world. It's more fun than studying and one delicious sip will stay in your memory far longer than any book. Wine tasting may well be work for professionals, but for you it should be an indulgence.

Read the label

The label tells you a great deal about the wine and sets it in context. It should feature the year the grapes were harvested, the region the wine comes from, its classification (for example, AC or vin de pays for a French wine – see page 70), the name and address of the producer and the alcohol level. Some, but not all, tell you the name of the grape variety. These days plenty of bottles, particularly from supermarkets, also have a back label which tells you such things as how sweet or dry the wine is, how long to keep it and what sort of food will go with it.

Look at the wine

Pour the wine into a wine glass so that it is a third full. A big tulip-shaped glass that is broad at the base and narrower at the top will help to concentrate the aromas of the wine. Tilt the glass against a white background so you can

Wine changes colour as it gets older. White wine is at its palest when it is young and gradually turns yellow. Red wine, on the other hand, is at its most intensely colourful in its youth and fades to brick red.

YOUNG   MATURE   YOUNG   MATURE

enjoy the range of colours in the wine from the centre to the rim. In general wines from hot countries and gutsy grape varieties have the deepest colour.

Smell the wine

Give the wine a vigorous swirl in the glass to release the locked-in aromas. Stick your nose right into the glass and inhale steadily and gently, as if you were smelling a flower.

These initial split seconds of inhalation will reveal all kinds of familiar and unfamiliar smells. Always interpret them in terms that mean something to you. If the smell reminds you of honey, or chocolate, or apples, or raspberries, then those descriptions are sure to be right for you. Remember, it's your nose that counts here. It doesn't matter if someone else interprets the smells differently – that's part of the pleasure of wine. It's only by reacting honestly to the taste and smell of a wine that you can build up a memory bank of flavours against which to judge future wines and to help you recognise wines you have already encountered.

essentials
TASTING BASICS

Nose is the name for the smell of the wine. Alternative terms are **aroma**, usually used of young wines, and **bouquet**, usually used for mature wines.

Palate is the taste of the wine in your mouth.

Sweetness or the lack of it is the first sensation as the wine hits the tip of your tongue. Sweetness always needs to be balanced by acidity or it will be cloying.

Acidity makes wine taste crisp. You notice its effect on the sides of your tongue. It must be balanced by sweetness, alcohol or body: a wine with too little of these and too much acidity will taste unpleasantly tart.

Tannin is the mouth-drying substance found in red wines. It contributes to the body and weight of the wine. Tannin must be balanced by fruit flavours and acidity to produce a good rounded flavour.

Alcohol is found in all wines, but levels vary from as little as 8% for a light German Riesling to around 14.5% for a rich, ripe Shiraz – and higher for fortified wines. High alcohol levels make wine feel rounder in your mouth.

Fruit flavour in wine comes from the grapes, yet wine seldom tastes of grapes. Instead flavours can resemble plums, strawberries, gooseberries or many other fruits – or indeed nuts, coffee beans, green leaves or biscuits.

Weight or **body** describes the different impressions of weight and size wines give in the mouth. This is what is referred to by the terms full-, medium- and light-bodied.

Length is the final factor to consider when assessing a wine. A wine with good length has something to say to all parts of your palate and leaves a lingering taste in your mouth after you swallow it or spit it out.

Balance, as you might have gathered from all the above, is the relationship between all elements of the wine: sweetness, acidity, fruit, body, tannin and alcohol. An unbalanced wine will taste as though it is lacking something – and it is.

At first you may find that you can't put a name to smells you do recognize or that there are too many smells to untangle in your mind, or even that the wine smells of nothing much at all. And it can be frustrating when a half-caught smell eludes you. Your nose tires quickly, so give it a break after a few seconds, then go back to the wine. It's worth jotting down a note of your thoughts before you forget them – a glance at the notes can bring the aromas flooding back weeks later.

Take a sip

At last! It's time to drink the wine. So take a decent-sized sip – enough to fill your mouth about a third full. The tongue can detect only very basic flavour elements: sweetness at the tip, acidity at the sides (saltiness too, but you won't find that in many wines) and bitterness at the back. The real business of tasting anything, not just wine, goes on in a cavity at the back of the mouth which is really part of the nose. The idea when tasting is to get the fumes from the wine in your mouth to rise up into this nasal cavity.

Evaluate the wine

First note any toughness, acidity and sweetness that the tongue detects. Draw a little air through your lips and suck it through the wine to help the aromas on their way and enjoy all the personality and flavour that the fumes impart. Now gently 'chew' the wine as if it were a piece of food, letting it coat your tongue, teeth, cheeks and gums.

Jot down first impressions, then the taste that develops after the wine has been in your mouth a few moments. Some flavours are upfront and unmistakable, others shift subtly, just out of reach. Don't try too hard to search out flavours and aromas; they are more likely come to you when you are relaxed. Tension, stress and anxiety all make it harder to taste what's in your mouth.

Swallow or spit it out

Why do wine tasters spit wine out after they have tasted it? Quite simply, it's the only way to taste a lot of wines and remain sober. If you are intending to drink the wine, there's no point in spitting, so go ahead and swallow it.

The aromas and flavours of blackcurrant and mint are typical of Cabernet Sauvignon from Coonawarra in South Australia.

But if you are tasting seriously or you are visiting a producer's cellar, spitting is the order of the day.

You don't need a special spittoon: just use a bucket and put some newspaper underneath for drips and misses. After spitting or swallowing, make a final note of any lingering aftertaste.

Blind tasting

It's very easy to imagine that you can detect a flavour in a wine if you expect it to be there. So, once you gain a bit of wine knowledge you may feel that reading the label affects your opinion of the wine when you taste it. This is the reason for tasting 'blind', the way professional tasters do, with the bottle and label carefully wrapped to conceal the wine's identity.

You'll need to get together with a group of people to organise a blind tasting because, obviously, somebody needs to know what's in the bottle. It can be great fun and teaches you a lot about both wine and your own senses of smell and taste.

Expert tips

Developing your tasting skills

Keep your nose alert Make a conscious effort to remember the smells you encounter in daily life and give them names. These form the basis of your tasting vocabulary and are the key to disentangling the elusive smells in wine.

Remember fruit flavours Fruit aromas and flavours are common in wine and it pays to be familiar with blackcurrants, blackberries, cherries, raspberries, strawberries and plums for red wines, and with lemons, limes, apples, apricots, peaches and tropical fruits for whites.

Make notes Keep a written record of the names of the wines you have tasted and your assessments of them. This doesn't need to be anything grand – two or three key words in your diary will do.

Make tasting a habit Whenever a glass of wine comes your way, pause to look at it, smell it and taste it. If you're having the wine with a meal, consider how the wine and food interact. Do they draw an extra dimension of flavour out of each other or does one knock the other flat?

Hold your own tastings Get together with some friends to compare a range of wines. A good way to start is by investigating the differences between two or three grape varieties. As you build your skills try comparing several wines made from the same variety. You could also taste a number of vintages of the same wine or the wines from one vintage made by several producers from a particular region.

Wine terms | **50 ways to describe wine**

There's more to describing wine than saying it's good or bad. Tasting terms are a way of sharing our perceptions of a wine's qualities; they should never be a secret code for experts. Fruit flavours are direct comparisons, so if I know the fruit, I will recognise the flavour you are talking about. The same goes for honey or nuts. These less obvious terms are useful too.

Aggressive A wine with acid that makes your gums sting or that dries up the back of your throat due to an excess of tannin.

Aromatic All wines have an aroma, but an aromatic wine is particularly pungent or *spicy*, and is usually from an aromatic grape variety like Gewürztraminer.

Astringent A wine in which the mouth-drying effect of tannin is very marked.

Big A full-bodied wine with lots of everything: fruit flavour, acid, tannin and alcohol.

Bold A wine with distinct, easily understood flavours.

Buttery A smell and taste of butter that results from maturing the wine in oak barrels.

Chewy Wine with a lot of tannin and strong flavour, but which is not *aggressive*.

Clean Wine free of bacterial and chemical faults. Also describes simple, refreshing wines.

Complex A wine that has layer upon layer of flavours.

Crisp A refreshing white with good acidity.

Deep Subtle, *rich*; allied to *complex*.

Dry Not at all *sweet*.

Dull A wine with no well-defined, pleasing flavours. Often a sign of too much exposure to oxygen.

Dusty A dry, slightly *earthy* taste sometimes found in reds. Can be very attractive if combined with good fruit.

Earthy A smell and taste of damp earth. Can be appealing in simple wines.

Fat Full-bodied, unctuous.

Firm Well balanced, well-defined wine; the opposite of *flabby*.

Flabby Lacking in acidity, feeble.

Focused A wine in which all the flavours are well defined.

Fresh Young wine, with lively fruit flavours and good acidity.

Full A wine with a weighty feel in the mouth.

Grassy A fresh-cut-grass aroma and taste, more accurately described as either capsicum, gooseberry or lime zest.

Green Can mean unripe, in which case it's pejorative. But green leaf flavours are common in cool-climate reds, and greenness in association with flavours such as gooseberries or apples, implies the fresh, tangy flavours found in some white wines.

Hard A red with a lot of tannin or a white with too much acid, but uncompromising rather than *aggressive*. One step beyond *firm*.

Jammy Red in which the fruit has the boiled, cooked flavours of jam.

Light Low alcohol or little body.

Meaty A heavy red wine with solid, chunky flavours. A few wines actually do taste of meat.

Minerally How you might imagine a lick of flint or chalk to taste. Common in wines from Germany and the Loire Valley in France.

Neutral Little distinctive flavour.

Oaky The slightly sweet vanilla flavour, the toastiness and the butteriness a wine acquires from new oak barrels.

Petrolly An attractive petrol-like smell that develops in mature wines made from Riesling.

Piercing Usually refers to high acidity. But fruit flavours can also be piercing if they're particularly vibrant.

Powerful A wine with plenty of everything, particularly alcohol.

Prickly Slight fizziness caused by residual carbon dioxide gas. Very refreshing in simple whites.

Rich Full, well-flavoured, with plenty of alcohol.

Ripe Wine made from well-ripened grapes has good fruit flavour. Unripe wines can taste *green*.

Rounded Any wine in which the flavour seems satisfyingly complete, with no unpleasant sharpness.

Soft A wine without harsh tannins or too much acidity, making it an easy-going drink.

Spicy Exotic fragrances and flavours common in Gewürztraminer; also the tastes of pepper, cinnamon or clove in reds such as Australian Shiraz. Spiciness can be an effect of oak aging.

Steely Good acidity and a wine that is firm and lean but not thin.

Stony A dry, chalky-white taste, like *minerally* but without the excitement.

Structured 'Plenty of structure' refers to a wine with a well-developed backbone of acid and tannin, but enough fruit to stand up to it.

Supple Both vigorous and smooth. A description of texture rather than flavour.

Sweet Not only a wine with high levels of sugar, but also the *rich* and *ripe* quality of some of the fruit flavours in many modern dry wines.

Tart A very sharp, acid taste like an unripe apple.

Thin, **lean**, **stringy** Terms for high-acid wine lacking in flavour.

Toasty A flavour like buttered toast that results from maturing a wine in oak barrels.

Upfront A wine that wears its heart on its sleeve: expect obvious flavours, not subtle ones.

How to spot a faulty wine

THE NUMBER OF poor wines in the shops is lower now than at any time in the history of wine, because winemaking is better understood now than ever before. Yet faulty bottles do crop up. You can spot faults in the same way as you can any wine flavour or quality, by using your senses of sight, smell and taste.

Use your eyes

Whatever its colour, wine should be clear and bright. Cloudy wine usually indicates bacterial spoilage, but it's extremely uncommon these days. Don't confuse cloudiness with shaken-up deposit: an aged red wine that has developed a dark, powdery or gritty deposit just needs to stand upright until the deposit settles again.

The colours of wines vary according to their grape variety and the climate in which they were made. But if a white wine you expect to be pale has a brownish-yellow tinge, or if a young red has a brownish tinge, then beware: it could be oxidised. Oxidised wine tastes dull and flat.

If wine has seeped past the cork, making the neck of the bottle sticky, then it probably hasn't been very well kept and air might have got in. This, too, can mean oxidised wine.

Use your nose

These smells are all tell-tale signs of trouble:

Sherry-like smells Only sherry should smell of sherry. Such smells on unfortified wines can indicate oxidation.

UNSIGHTLY BUT NOT FAULTY

Pieces of cork floating in your wine glass are nothing to do with cork-tainted wine. They are unsightly but have no effect on the flavour.

White crystals often form on the cork and at the bottom of bottles of white wine. These natural deposits, called tartrates, are harmless and do not alter the taste of the wine.

Sediment often develops in red wines after a few years in the bottle. This is best dealt with by decanting.

Vinegary smells If it smells like vinegar, then that is what it is turning into.

Rotten eggs This horrible, horrible smell of hydrogen sulphide can form during fermentation and is a sign of poor winemaking.

Mouldy, musty smells This is 'corked' wine, caused by a contaminated cork. A little cork taint may just dull the wine but not make it undrinkable.

Use your taste buds

Your palate should normally confirm what your nose has already told you – but sometimes a fault will show more on the nose than on the palate, or vice versa. Use nose and palate in conjunction when judging a wine.

 Wine terms | **Sulphur**

Sometimes a freshly-opened bottle of wine has a distinct sulphury whiff of **burnt matches**. This comes from **sulphur dioxide**, an all-purpose antiseptic and anti-oxidant used in almost every winery in the world. It is added to the wine at the bottling stage to ensure that it keeps absolutely fresh in bottle. In time the sulphur dioxide is absorbed by the wine, and then you won't taste or smell it. Excess sulphur dioxide will usually dissipate after a few minutes, particularly if you decant the wine to get some air to it.

Drinking wine in a restaurant

THE KEY HERE IS: if in doubt, ask. This applies regardless of the sort of restaurant you're in. If there's a well-informed sommelier (that's the person who is in charge of the wine) and the wine list seems to have been put together with care, then he or she will be only too pleased to tell you anything you want to know – and will probably have some suggestions about which wines will go particularly well with the food you have chosen.

A lot of restaurants, of course, have neither a particularly good wine list, nor a decent sommelier. If the list doesn't tell you the vintage, or the producer, or some other vital piece of information about a wine, ask to see the bottle. At least you can then make your own mind up.

The quality of a wine list is not measured by its length. A short, well-chosen list is often better, as is one that specialises in the wines of one region.

Ordering your wine

Okay, you've decided what you're going to eat, and you've had a look at the wine list and decided what price you want to pay. What you don't know is what any of it tastes

Good restaurants, bad restaurants

A good restaurant for wine
- Gives full details of the wines on the wine list
- Offers wines that have been carefully chosen to go with the food
- Will replace a faulty bottle with good grace
- Serves good house wine and a selection of interesting wines by the glass.

A bad restaurant for wine
- Gives no specific information about the wines
- Challenges your judgement if you complain
- Has uninformed or overbearing staff
- Tries to make you spend more than you want to.

like. The wine waiter approaches. How do you begin? Try something like this: 'Oh, hello. Now, we're both having the duck, but I think it'll have to be a white, because my friend/lover/nephew/boss doesn't drink red. There's a Hunter Valley Semillon here – is that oaked? What would you recommend?'

You've given the waiter all the clues he or she needs – food, style and price range – to make an appropriate suggestion. And now you've broken the ice you can come to a final decision calmly rather than in a state of blind panic. The worst thing, if you don't know what to choose, is to sit staring in terror at the wine list, and refuse to ask because you think you'll lose face. You won't.

However, it is a good idea to make a preliminary choice before you seek advice: if you don't like the advice you get, it will leave you with something to fall back on.

When the bottle comes and is shown to you, check it. Sometimes the wrong wine arrives because somebody misheard. Sometimes the vintage has changed, and nobody's told you. If it's not the vintage you ordered, query it. If you don't want the replacement, choose something else.

When the waiter pours the wine, sniff it and taste it. You're checking to see if it's faulty, not if you like it. Take your time. If you suspect it might be faulty, express your doubts, take another taste and ask the waiter to taste it. If it is faulty he or she should immediately take the bottle away and replace it.

This is where most of the problems with wine waiters arise. Bad wine waiters refuse to accept that a faulty wine is faulty. Bad customers insist that a wine is faulty when there's nothing wrong with it – it may just be unfamiliar.

If you have a disastrous experience (and everyone who eats in restaurants has a bad wine waiter story) don't pick a row: it will spoil the evening. A quiet, reasoned complaint to the manager at the end of the meal will do more good. And if you've had bad service, don't leave a tip.

 | ## Expert tips
Top 10 restaurant tactics

1. Try a glass of house wine first – it allows you to take your time when choosing the wine and if it's good you could stick with it.

2. Order water to quench your thirst so you can savour the wine.

3. Discuss your choice of wine with the wine waiter if there is one. Don't treat him or her as an enemy – or a hired slave.

4. If you're going to have two bottles, don't blow your budget on the first.

5. Don't worry too much about matching the wine to your food: New World Cabernet Sauvignons and Merlots are good all-round reds; New World Chardonnays and Semillons are useful whites; and Alsace whites go well with a great variety of dishes.

6. On an uninspiring list, opt for wines from Australia or South America – they are the most likely to be reliable and good value.

7. Take a chance on up-and-coming regions of Italy, Spain or Portugal – they could well be the best value on the list.

8. Feel the temperature of the bottle when it arrives. If the wine is too warm, whether it's red or white, ask for an ice bucket; and if it gets too cold, don't feel you have to keep it in the bucket just because the waiter has put it there.

9. Don't be bullied by over-assiduous waiters – make sure the bottle is within your reach and top up your glasses when you want to.

10. Enjoy yourself: you're the one who's paying.

A good restaurant will aim to help you enjoy the wine it serves – decent glasses are a good start.

Matching food and wine

GOOD WINE IS TASTY on its own, but to get the best out of wine you need a group of friends around, and a bite to eat. So, how do you go about choosing the wine for the meal? The pleasures of eating and drinking operate on so many levels that there's far more to perfect wine-food partnerships than clinical flavour matching. If you're in the mood for Champagne then don't let anyone stop you drinking it, whatever you're eating; and if the spirit of place, or the weather, or the company you're in begs for a particular wine, go for it.

Basic principles

Wine affects the flavour of food; food affects the flavour of wine – pretty obvious, I suppose. When the fundamental characteristics of the wine and the food are in harmony, the flavours of both should sing out. Sometimes a well-judged contrast does the trick just as well as a perfect match. Frankly, most combinations are perfectly enjoyable and a few are sensationally good, but a real mismatch can take the fun out of both the food and the wine.

Fortunately, it's easy to avoid disastrous pairings. Don't drink dry wine with sweet food – the wine will taste unpleasantly thin and acidic – and stick to red meat if the wine is a high-tannin red, such as Barolo from Italy, Dão or Bairrada from Portugal, or red Bordeaux. And that's about it. Now you can get on with looking for combinations that bring out the best in both the wine and the food. I've made a few suggestions in the tables opposite and over the page, but these are the main things to bear in mind:

Weight As well as matching the taste of the wine to the flavour of the food, it's a good idea to match the weight (or body) of the wine to the intensity of that flavour. A heavy, alcoholic wine suits hefty food; choose a light wine for delicate dishes.

Acidity The acidity of the food should balance that of the wine. High-acid flavours, such as tomato or lemon, need matching acidity in the wine. You can also use an acidic wine to cut through a creamy or oily dish, but make sure the wine has plenty of flavour.

Sweetness With desserts and puddings, find a wine that is as sweet as or sweeter than the food. Some savoury foods, such as carrots, onions and parsnips, taste slightly sweet, and if they are prominent in the dish a really ripe-fruited wine will work well.

Age/maturity A mature wine will have developed a complex taste and aroma over the years. To get the most enjoyment out of it, keep the food simple – plain grilled or roast meat is ideal.

Sauces and seasonings Always bear these in mind. It may be more important to match the wine to a rich sauce or spicy seasonings than to the main ingredient.

Oak A heavily oaked wine can ride roughshod over food that isn't richly flavoured.

essentials

WINE'S WORST ENEMIES

Artichokes, asparagus, spinach, kippers and **mackerel, salsas** and **vinegars**, and **chocolate** can all flatten the flavours of wines. If you want to drink wine with these foods, the general rule for reds is to avoid very tannic wines and go for juicy young ones instead; or choose whites with plenty of fruit and fresh acidity.

With mackerel try a dry fino sherry, and with chocolate go for fortified Muscats, the Italian sparkling wine Asti or perhaps some port. Vinegary dressings and salsas need a match for their acidity, so team them with Sauvignon Blanc or dry Riesling.

Eggs can be tricky to match with wine. Choose light, unoaked Chardonnays or neutral whites – oaky and very fruity ones don't work so well. Only the very lightest reds, such as Beaujolais, go well with eggs.

Red wine and food: some suggestions for the wine styles described on pages 8–15.

	Juicy, fruity reds	Silky, strawberryish reds	Intense, blackcurranty reds	Spicy, warm-hearted reds	Low-tannin, mouthwatering, sweet-sour reds	Tannic, mouthwatering, sweet-sour reds
EXCELLENT MATCH	Roast or grilled red meats	Red meat in rich sauce, e.g. boeuf bourguignon	Roast or grilled red meats – especially lamb	Peppered steak	Pizza	Rich game dishes
	Barbecues	Roast game birds	Venison	Sausages	Lasagne	Warming, herby stews
	Roast or fried chicken	Roast or grilled red meats	Duck and goose	Warming, herby stews	Tomato-based dishes	Roast or grilled red meats
	Ham	Chicken in red wine sauce or cooked with garlic	Roast chicken and turkey	Duck and goose	Spaghetti Bolognese	
	Roast pork			Roast or grilled red meats	Cold meats and salamis	
	Spicy food		Cold roast beef	Venison stew	Roast pork	
	Indian and Tex-Mex food	Substantial fish, such as grilled salmon or tuna		Anything barbecued	Garlicky and herby dishes	Roast chicken or turkey with stuffing
	Cold meats and pâtés		Red meat in rich sauce	Indian food		
OK MATCH	Grilled fish	Roast pork		Tex-Mex food	Roast or grilled red meats	
	Creamy or cheesy sauces			Herbs and spices		
		Rich, lightly spiced Oriental dishes		Chilli con carne		
	Spaghetti Bolognese and lasagne			Spaghetti Bolognese	Grilled fish	
	Pizza			Salami		
	Tomato-based dishes			Roast chicken or turkey with stuffing		
DISASTER WARNING	**Only the standard warning that goes for all dry reds – avoid sweet foods.**	**These wines lose their charm with fiery spicy food.**	**They overwhelm fish, taste bitter with tomatoes and spicy foods, and don't suit cold pork or chicken.**	**These are food-loving wines, but they will swamp delicate food.**	**No problems – these wines are real all-rounders.**	**These wines only come into their own with robust, meaty meals. They clash with cold pork or chicken.**

White wine and food: some suggestions for the wine styles described on pages 8–9 and 16–22.

	Bone-dry, neutral whites	Green, tangy whites	Intense, nutty whites	Ripe, toasty whites	Aromatics	Other wine styles
EXCELLENT MATCH → OK MATCH	Plainly cooked fish and shellfish	Anything in tomato sauce, including shellfish	Creamy and buttery sauces	Grilled or baked salmon and tuna	Thai and Chinese food	**Rosés** that are dry and fruity make excellent partners for a whole range of dishes from delicate fish to rich spicy food, but, as they're light, steer away from heavy meaty dishes.
	Grilled chicken breasts	Tomatoes	Plain grilled white fish	Creamy and buttery sauces	Smoked fish	
		Pizza	Grilled or roast chicken and turkey	Grilled or roast chicken and turkey	Duck and goose	
	Spaghetti carbonara	Indian food			Rich pâtés	
	Quiche	Salads with sharp dressing	Smoked salmon	Barbecues	Pork	**Dry sparkling wines** are good all-rounders too, and particularly good with shellfish and smoked fish. Champagne with oysters is a classic luxury match, although non-vintage Champagne is more suitable than richer, more expensive vintage.
	Salads	Sushi	Spaghetti carbonara	Pheasant or rabbit	Quiche	
	Cajun and Tex-Mex food	Goat's cheese	Grilled or baked salmon and tuna	Spaghetti carbonara	Anything that combines a lot of strong flavours – e.g. Asian food, mixed charcuterie or smorgasbord	
	Salami	South-East Asian food	Seafood in a white wine and cream sauce	Seafood in a white wine and cream sauce		
	Pork	Tex-Mex food			Indian food	**Tangy, fortified wines** are good with pre-dinner snacks such as olives and nuts, go well with soups and are the classic partner to Spanish tapas.
	Thai and Chinese food	Chinese Szechuan food			Anything cooked with fresh ginger	
	Cold meats	Grilled or baked salmon and tuna	Pork			
	Tomato-based dishes			Cold pork and chicken		
	Pizza		Pheasant or rabbit			**Warming, fortified wines** suit cheese and chocolate.
	Creamy and buttery sauces			Smoked fish		
				Mildly spiced food		**Golden, sweet wines** go with both sweet food and blue cheese.
DISASTER WARNING	**Avoid pairing any dry white with sweet food, but otherwise you can't go wrong with these wines.**	**These wines work with all sorts of hard-to-match foods, but they don't suit simply cooked red meats.**	**For all their intensity, these are subtly flavoured wines, and spices will destroy all that subtlety.**	**Heavily oaked wines overwhelm delicate fish – but they won't stand up to too much spice or acidity.**	**Aromatics are great food wines, but they're better suited to complex dishes than simple ones.**	

Sense of place

My best memories of sublime wine and food partnerships come from picnics I have had while travelling in France and Italy. I'll stop in the villages of Tuscany or southern France to pick up bread, cheese and tomatoes, buy wine straight from the local winemaker's barrel and gulp it all down ten minutes later at the side of a country lane. Wine and food will never taste better than this.

The magic resides in the simplicity of the meal and the joy of basking in the same sunlight that is ripening the vines. There's a lesson to be learnt from this for wine and food matching at home. Regional wines and foods aren't necessarily ideal matches from a scientific point of view, but a technical approach takes the fun out of the wine and the food. It's much better to make a bit of a holiday of your meal and think along the lines of southern French wine with Provençal food or a light Italian red with pizza.

International cuisines

Wine and food are both international travellers these days and they pick up new friends wherever they go. Many of the food styles popular around the world today grew up in cultures that don't have wine in their repertoire. Rich and spicy Chinese, Thai, Vietnamese, Indian, African and Mexican dishes and the mixed cuisines of Fusion Food and Pacific Rim cooking demand wines with a character that the traditional wine cultures of Europe never had to provide but which fruit-driven modern styles deliver.

Nevertheless, some European classics *do* deliver the fruit: Alsace wines, particularly Gewurztraminer, and German Riesling. Riesling from any country is a good choice, as are the intense Sauvignon Blancs from New Zealand and South Africa. Juicy fruity reds bear up well and powerful California Zinfandel is a good choice.

Wine and cheese

I'm really not sure why cheese is always seen as a natural partner for wine. Only occasionally do I come across an

Expert tips

Restaurant dilemmas

If you're in a restaurant and everyone is ordering different food, even the most resourceful expert is going to have difficulty choosing one ideal wine. In this situation, the traditional combination of a bottle of white and a bottle of red should see you through.

exciting combination. The enduring cliché, perpetuated by a host of back labels, that red wine is the wine for cheese, is even more perplexing. If it has dissuaded you from drinking white wine with cheese up to now, I'm afraid you've been missing out, because white is in general a better partner for it.

Red wines are okay for hard cheeses like mild Cheddar or Gouda and bland ones such as Mozzarella. For mature Cheddar and other strong hard cheeses you need a powerful red like Rhône Syrah or Australian Shiraz, or even port. Goat's cheese is better off with the Loire Valley white wine Sancerre or other wines made from Sauvignon Blanc. Ripe cheeses like Brie or Camembert are hostile to most wine flavours, but sparkling wines can tame them. Strong blue cheeses call for sweet wines: the classic combinations are port with Stilton and Bordeaux's sweet white Sauternes with Roquefort.

Vegetarian dishes

The clean, bright, appley flavours of Pinot Blanc from Alsace and the simple fruitiness and low tannins of Grenache and Tempranillo make them good all-rounders for modern vegetarian cooking. Dry rosé is a good idea, too. Anything spicy calls for fruity and acidic reds and whites. So do tomato-based sauces. Cream and cheese sauces need softer wines: Sémillon or ripe, toasty Chardonnay would be good. Salads with vinegary dressings can be murder on wine. Go for tangy whites, such as dry Riesling or Sauvignon Blanc.

Wine and health

THE IMAGE OF WINE as a healthy drink is both an ancient and a very modern one. Wine was once highly prized for its medicinal qualities, largely because it was more reliably hygienic than water. It made a reasonable antiseptic when little else was available, and a good base for medicines. Some doctors went further, and recommended particular wines for particular ailments, but empirical evidence must have been somewhat lacking for this.

The damaging effects of alcohol have been known for a long time, too, and the anti-alcohol lobby has tried for years to persuade us that all alcohol is bad for us. However, there's now a wealth of medical evidence to suggest that moderate consumption of alcohol, particularly in the form of wine, is actually better for most people's health than total abstinence.

Health benefits

The main research finding is that wine reduces the likelihood of dying from a heart attack, stroke or other form of vascular disease. It does this by helping to prevent clogged arteries and blood clots.

Some of the benefits are due to the alcohol in the wine. Alcohol acts as an anticoagulant, which eases blood flow and prevents clots forming. It boosts HDL – or 'good'

RECOMMENDED AMOUNTS

Governments set guidelines for sensible drinking limits, but these aren't consistent worldwide. Most are in the range of 28–40 grams of alcohol per day for men (equivalent to two to three 125ml glasses of wine containing 13.5% alcohol), and half to two-thirds that amount for women.

cholesterol – which actually cleans fatty deposits out of our arteries, and reduces LDL, the 'bad' cholesterol that puts them there in the first place.

Wine has an extra trick up its sleeve in the form of powerful anti-oxidants, which reduce the amount of fatty LDL deposits that can stick to the walls of our arteries. This benefit was originally attributed only to red wines, but subsequent research has shown that white wines are also effective. It also appears that wine may reduce the risk of some cancers and aid mental alertness into old age. And of course, we don't need researchers to tell us about the relaxing effects of a glass or two at the end of the day.

Moderate consumption

All advocates of wine as a healthy beverage stress that the benefits of wine come only with moderate, regular consumption. Excessive amounts of alcohol increase the likelihood of many health problems, including all those that moderate consumption can guard against. In addition, alcohol is not recommended for people suffering from certain diseases, and pregnant women in particular should take medical advice regarding alcohol.

Individuals should talk to their doctors and make up their own minds, but my feelings on the matter are simple. Drink water for your thirst and enjoy good wine for its flavour. If you're not drinking enough to harm yourself, then the pleasure and sense of wellbeing that wine adds to your life are benefits enough.

In 1999 US producers won the right to allude to the health benefits of wine on their labels. Laurel Glen was at the forefront of the campaign.

Buying and storing wine

I HAVE A CHAOTIC jumble of bottles under the stairs in my house, and stray bottles tucked into odd corners in the kitchen, the box room and behind the TV. But however much wine I accumulate, it's never going to stop me dropping into my local wine shop to browse, have a chat and pick up a bottle for the evening. This is the way we buy most of our wine these days, not by the case, not for laying down, just as part of our daily shopping.

Where to buy wine

Shopping for wine can be so much more, though, than a dash to your local store: it can be a pleasure and a leisure pursuit in itself. For sheer range of choice, the best thing to do is stay at home. Seriously. The Internet has revolutionised wine buying. Plenty of established merchants and Internet-only wine 'e-tailers' have websites which you can browse at leisure, comparing prices and digging out far more information on individual wines than you'll be likely to find on a shop shelf.

Of course, it's just an advanced version of traditional mail-order shopping, which has been a mainstay of wine retailing for years. Both methods have the advantage that you don't need to worry about carting the wine home and, more importantly, give you access to a vast number of wines not available in your local area.

What they lack is the quiet meditative atmosphere of a really good wine shop – the cool, even slightly musty air, the calming lighting, the stillness. It slows the pulse rate and gives you the space and time to browse, choose with care and dream about bottles you will never be able to afford. These are all signs of a shop that stores the wine in appropriate conditions and has knowledgeable staff. You may pay a bit more for your wine here, but this is where to come when you need inspiration.

Most shops offer a discount on a 12-bottle case, and this is the minimum quantity you can buy from many Internet and mail order merchants. You don't have to buy a whole case of the same wine: you can usually order a selection of bottles (called a mixed case).

If you're interested in wine 'futures' or *en primeur* offers – that is, investing in wine that is still at the winery or château and not yet bottled – make sure you go to a merchant with a good track record in handling such transactions and with a solid trading base in other wines.

Getting information

Wines are reviewed on TV, on the radio, in newspapers and magazines and on dedicated wine websites, but sharing your experiences with friends is one of the best ways of gathering recommendations. Some shops have informative cards on the shelves and many wines have detailed descriptions on the back label.

Most modern homes aren't equipped with a cellar for storing wine. If an understairs cupboard just won't do you could take the plunge and install a purpose-built Spiral Cellar underneath your house.

Expert tips
Good shops, bad shops

A good wine shop
- has clued-up staff and plenty of information about the wines
- is cool and not too brightly lit
- is prepared to advise you to buy a cheaper wine
- holds regular wine tastings
- offers a mixture of young and mature wines.

A bad wine shop
- has uninformed staff
- has wine standing upright on the shelves that has been gathering dust and gently cooking for months on end
- has pushy staff who try to make you buy a more expensive wine than you intended
- only sells brand-name wines
- gives more space to beers, cigarettes, groceries and snacks.

This is the kind of wine shop I enjoy. It's interesting, imaginatively designed and well stocked; the wines are well stored, the lighting is not too strong and there's a tempting range of samples for customers to try.

All wine merchants publish lists of the wines they stock. The simplest name the wines and their prices, and give details of the merchant's terms of business. More ambitious lists review all the wines (sometimes with the whiff of marketing hype) and may include details about the merchant's pet wine regions and winemakers.

Most merchants hold regular wine tastings. Some are formal occasions, others simply a matter of opening a few bottles for customers to sample during shop hours. Surprisingly few merchants will pressure you to buy any of the wines being tasted.

Getting good service

If you want to know about any of the wines in a shop, ask. Enthusiastic and knowledgeable staff are usually bursting to tell you about their wines. If none of the staff knows anything about the wines, or you get the impression that they are blustering, it's probable that they don't handle the wines too carefully either. Shop elsewhere.

However well a merchant does handle the wines, it's impossible to guarantee that every bottle is fault-free. Most shops will happily exchange the wine for a replacement bottle if you suspect a fault after opening the wine.

It's worth buying regularly from one merchant. Let them know which wines you liked and which you weren't so keen on. The more a merchant knows about your preferences, the better he or she will be able to guide you.

Buying direct from the producer

Some châteaux and wineries are only too happy to sell wine from the cellar door or by mail order. For some, it's the only way they sell it. If you're visiting, call first to check opening times and if necessary to make an appointment. But beware: even in this age of online shopping you can still run up against archaic trade barriers. Wherever you live you'll generally have to pay a customs duty on wine shipped to you from abroad. And in some US states, it is actually illegal for consumers to buy wine direct from outside the state.

Storing wine

Very few of us have a big, dark, cool cellar under our house where we can lay down wines to mature for years on end. Just as well then, that plenty of modern wines aren't designed to benefit from extended aging anyway. It's still worth keeping a few bottles in a rack to save running down to the shop all the time. Store the wine you buy out of direct sunlight and away from major heat sources and it will be happy for a few months.

However, a fiercely tannic red will only reveal its sweeter nature after several years, and many high-quality white wines develop with time. If you just keep them standing about the house for years on end, the light, warmth and dry air will conspire to ruin the wine.

You need somewhere fairly cool and humid that isn't subject to a huge leap in temperature every time the central heating fires up; darkness (you could drape a blanket over the wines); and lack of vibration. And lie the wine on its side to keep the corks damp and swollen, which preserves the airtight seal.

An understairs cupboard is a good storage place. Failing that, you could try the back of a wardrobe or a bottom drawer. For perfect storage conditions you could buy a temperature- and humidity-controlled cabinet or even have a cellar installed under your house, but both options are expensive. Alternatively, pay for your wine merchant to store the wines. Make sure that you receive a stock certificate and that your cases are clearly identified and stored separately from the merchant's own stock.

 Wine terms | **Bin ends**

Bin ends are simply leftovers: they're the last bottles of the old vintage, and the wine merchant wants to clear them out to make room for the new vintage. Or the merchant bought too much of a particular wine, and wants to shift it. Or they're just odds and ends that are taking up space. Either way, they may be offered at reduced prices. Often they're a bargain – but there's always a risk they may be past their best.

Understanding wine labels

A WINE LABEL is not just the attractive final touch to the bottle or an advertisement for the producer's sense of style, it is a guide to the contents of the bottle. If you consider some of the things I've been saying about wine, you will be able to form a pretty good idea of the information you would like to find printed on the label.

You can see for yourself whether the wine is white or red. Next I would want to know which grapes the wine is made from, where they were grown, who made the wine and when. With this information, you'll be in a position to know what you're getting.

It seems simple enough to offer this passport-style information, and many wine labels lay it all out with commendable clarity. Others can seem a bit obscure, though really it's only a question of understanding a little more about how the world of wine works.

Impostors

Rules about how wines may be described on labels are tighter than ever. It's true that sparkling wines from America, North and South, can call themselves 'Champagne' as long as they're not shipped to Europe, but there has been progress. Australia is phasing out the misleading use of classic French wine names – Chablis, Sauternes and so on – for its own wines.

What we have to look out for now is wines from unfashionable areas being repackaged to look like wines from fashionable ones. It's quite simple and quite legal: you take your Eastern European white and red, give them a brand name like Kangaroo Creek and leave the details of where they were made for the small print.

No, it's not very terrible. And as long as the wine tastes as modern as the packaging, I can't entirely condemn it. But it's a shame that they think we'll only buy their wine if it looks like something else. Especially when experience shows we'll buy anything, if it's good enough.

What will it taste like?

The simplest labels to understand are those that state the grape variety. Most labels of New World wines do this, although there's also a fashion for naming top-class wines after a bin number or a vat number or the vineyard or the proprietor's daughter. But in such cases the back label often gives the game away and tells you the grapes used.

The grape variety is the biggest clue the label gives to the taste of the wine. The next biggest is the place. If you've read as far as this you'll know that Sauvignon Blanc from New Zealand has a particular style and flavour; when you see a bottle you know more or less what to expect.

In the case of European wines, the grape varieties are not often stated. However, they tend to be defined by the rules that apply in the region that the wine is named after. That's why I've put together the Appellation Decoder on pages 138–40 to link classic wines with their grape varieties. Because what you need to be able to do, when looking at a wine label, is put it in context.

Red Rioja, for example, is made principally from a blend of Tempranillo and Garnacha (Grenache) grapes, so it has a particular flavour; red Bordeaux is principally a blend of Cabernet Sauvignon, Merlot and Cabernet Franc, and has a different flavour. It is illegal to grow Tempranillo and Grenache in Bordeaux and call the result Bordeaux.

I mentioned the term terroir a while back. Terroir is the basis of the French appellation system. As I said, in the French view, terroir is what makes each vineyard different from its neighbour. So it makes sense to take an area that shares more or less the same terroir and give it one name (or appellation), then take another area with basically a slightly different terroir, and give it another name. Even if the grapes are the same, the style of the wine should be different. Five appellations in the northern Rhône Valley produce red wines based on the Syrah grape but each has (in theory) its own unique character.

Wine terms

Dry, medium or sweet?

For wines from all countries except Germany, you can generally assume that the wine is dry unless otherwise stated.

FRANCE
Dry is **sec**; **demi-sec** is off-dry. **Doux** or **moelleux** is sweet; **liquoreux** very sweet. For Champagne, **brut** is the driest – **extra dry** is, confusingly, less dry. **Demi-sec** (or **rich**) is fairly sweet. Beware of wines from appellations which apply specifically to sweet wines, such as Sauternes; these make no mention on the label of the fact that the wine is sweet.

ITALY
Dry is **secco**, medium-dry is **semisecco**. Medium-sweet is **abboccato** or **amabile**. Sweet wines are **dolce**.

SPAIN
The terms are **seco**, **semi-seco** and **dulce**.

GERMANY
Wines here tend to be at least slightly sweet unless otherwise stated. **Trocken** is dry, **Halbtrocken** off-dry.

AUSTRIA
Dry wines are far more common here than in Germany. Austrian sweet styles are, in ascending order of sweetness, **Spätlese**, **Auslese**, **Beerenauslese**, **Ausbruch**, **Trockenbeerenauslese** and **Eiswein**.

Is it any good?

The most pressing question, the one that none of the information on the label will answer directly, is whether the wine is good, bad or indifferent. And, try as they might, official classification systems don't help much.

The most basic way of classifying wine is by the place of origin. Most New World countries are settling for something like the US AVA (American Viticultural Area) system. Each area is supposed to be homogeneous in some way – climate, for example – but in practice many AVAs have boundaries that simply follow county lines. This sort of system guarantees the geographical origin of the wine, but carries no quality connotations.

All the European systems are based to some extent on the concept of terroir. To ensure that the intrinsic character of each region's wine is maintained, it is deemed necessary to regulate all aspects of wine production.

The most strictly regulated wines in France (and each European country has an equivalent classification – see the box below) are Appellation Contrôlée wines. The words Appellation Contrôlée on a label are not, however, a guarantee of quality – instead they guarantee that the wine possesses the character of the region, and has been made in accordance with the rules of that region. This is why it is illegal to grow any old grape varieties in Bordeaux and claim the Bordeaux appellation for the wine. For VDQS wines the rules are slightly more relaxed; the vin de pays rules are positively slack; and vins de table can be pretty much anything that won't kill you.

If you want a guarantee of quality, in the Old World and in the New, you have to go by the name of the producer. A poor producer can follow all the rules and come up with poor wine; a good producer will make creditable wine in almost any circumstances.

essentials

WINE CLASSIFICATIONS: EUROPE

The French appellation system is the most widely known system of quality control. Other European countries have roughly equivalent gradings, though some have more categories. Quality within any of the bands is not consistent and a good example of a simple wine will be better than a poorly made wine that has complied with the rules to achieve a higher status.

	France	Italy	Portugal	Spain	Germany
Special-quality wine	No category	Denominazione di Origine Controllata e Garantita (DOCG)	No category	Denominación de Origen Calificada (DOC)	Qualitätswein mit Prädikat (QmP) – divided into 6 styles
Quality wine	Appellation d'Origine Contrôlée (AC/AOC) or Vin Délimité de Qualité Supérieure (VDQS)	Denominazione di Origine Controllata (DOC)	Denominação de Origem Controlada (DOC) or Indicação de Proviniência Regulamentada (IPR)	Denominación de Origen (DO)	Qualitätswein bestimmter Anbaugebiete (QbA)
Regional wine	Vin de pays	Indicazione Geografica Tipica (IGT)	Vinho regional	Vino de la tierra or vino comarcal	Landwein
Basic wine	Vin de table	Vino da tavola	Vinho de mesa	Vino de mesa	Tafelwein

Which producer?

The producer, as I said earlier, is the company that makes the wine. It has control over the choice of grapes, who makes the wine and how, and so is responsible for the quality of the wine. High quality doesn't necessarily mean a high price: one thing that marks out a good producer is how much better the wines are than poorly made or unexciting wines of a similar price. You'll find a list of wines from recommended producers in each of the chapters in The World of Wine on pages 74–137.

There are thousands and thousands of wine producers in the world and you can't hope to know all of them, or even all of the good ones, even in one country. If you know nothing about the producer of the wine then buying it is a risk. It's a matter of taking advice and experimenting to find producers whose wines you like.

Easily recognised brand-name wines offer a safe route out of the producer maze. The quality of these wines is generally good these days, although they can be over-priced. But if I buy a brand name, I'm buying a non-specific wine, blended to a happy-medium sort of a taste. It will probably be perfectly nice, and reliably so, but it's unlikely to be exciting.

Back labels

Buying wine would be far easier if the label told you how the wine tasted; some back labels do. Many retailers also have helpful systems for grading each of the wines they sell on a scale from bone dry to very sweet for whites, and from light to full-bodied for reds. Back labels can tell you how oaky the wine is and which grape varieties were used to make it. Or they can tell you whether the wine is suitable for aging and what foods will go well with it. But they can also be complete waffle.

It's up to you to make the distinction between useful information and the interventions of an enthusiastic marketing department. Treat back-label information as a general guide to the wine and don't let yourself be drawn in by florid accounts of the winemaking.

Expert tips
Five things to look for on the label

1. **Estate bottled** This should mean that the grapes have been grown, made into wine and bottled in one place, which should in turn mean that the wine has been made with pride and has individuality. On French labels the equivalent terms are *mis en bouteille au château/domaine/à la propriété*. Australia has a tradition of making high quality blends of wines from different estates and regions, so the term is less significant there.

2. **Cru** A French wine term used to indicate a village or vineyard of high quality, particularly in the regions of Bordeaux, Burgundy and Alsace.

3. **Traditional method** Sparkling wine made the same way as Champagne. *Méthode traditionelle* in French.

4. **Old vines** The grapes that grow on old vines tend to have more concentrated juice and so make more densely flavoured wines than those from youngsters. The French phrase is *vieilles vignes*.

5. **The vintage** No, I'm not suggesting that you become a vintage bore. But at the very least, knowing how old the wine is will give you an idea of whether it will taste young or mature.

TALUS
ZINFANDEL

Zinfandel is the ultimate pizza and burger wine. This Zinfandel has the spicy, berry-like fruit that jumps out of your glass. I aged it just long enough in oak barrels to tame some of the intensity of the fruit without losing its zest. Try it with Mexican food, hearty tomato-sauced dishes or stews.

Melissa Bates, Talus Winemaker

The back label is often where you'll find what you really want know about a wine, but bear in mind that this information is also a sales pitch.

Expert tips
Five things to be wary of on a label

1. **Reserve** In some countries (notably Spain and Italy) reserve wines are matured in oak for longer than the standard wines and a full set of rules is in force. Elsewhere the term might be used to indicate this style of wine, but then again it might mean nothing at all.

2. **Supérieur** Surely a superior wine is better? Sorry, wrong. This French term and its Italian equivalent **superiore** indicate only that the wine has a slightly higher alcohol content than the ordinary wine of the same name.

3. **Grand vin** In Bordeaux, Grand Vin indicates that it is the main wine of the property, as opposed to a second wine. It does not mean 'great wine'.

4. **South-Eastern Australia** No, there's nothing wrong with this – just bear in mind that South-Eastern Australia includes the vast majority of Australia's wine-producing areas. So while it might look like a specific appellation, it's not as specific as all that.

5. **Anything that claims to be special, exceptional, classic, a limited release, from the founder's bin...** Just ignore these terms and stick to the basics of who, what, when and where in deducing the likely quality of the wine.

1. The name of the producer
2. The name of the wine
3. The appellation – quality classification and place of origin (French wine regulations expect this name to tell you all you need to know about the taste of the wine. This appellation in the Loire Valley, for example, is actually for sweet wines made from Chenin Blanc grapes, and nothing else on the label will tell you that)
4. The year the grapes were harvested (the vintage)
5. This means the wine was bottled on the producer's estate and suggests a higher than average level of quality
6. The quantity of wine in the bottle – 750ml is the standard bottle size in the EU.
7. The alcohol content

Spanish and Italian labels work in much the same way as French ones.

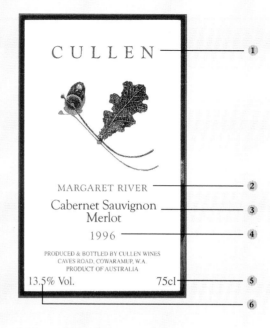

1. The name of the producer
2. The region the wine comes from
3. The vintage
4. The village and vineyard – the wine comes from Oberhaus (the -er after the name of the village means that the vineyard 'belongs' to that place); and the grapes were grown in the Brücke vineyard
5. The grape variety
6. The ripeness classification of the grapes (see the box, below)
7. The alcohol content
8. The quantity of wine in the bottle
9. The overall quality classification of the wine
10. This means the wine was bottled by the producer

1. The name of the producer
2. The region in which the grapes were grown
3. The grape varieties (the predominant variety is named first)
4. The vintage
5. The quantity of wine in the bottle
6. The alcohol content

essentials GERMAN WINE STYLES

Qualitätswein mit Prädikat (the top overall classification for German wine) comes in six styles or grades, defined by the ripeness of the grapes used.

Kabinett The lightest QmP wine. It will be semi-sweet unless labelled as **Halbtrocken** (off-dry) or **Trocken** (dry).
Spätlese ('late-picked') Many are sweetish, though Halbtrocken and Trocken versions are also made.
Auslese ('selected') Wine made from selected bunches of very ripe grapes. Most are fully sweet but some are dry.
Beerenauslese ('selected berries') Luscious sweet wine made from selected single grapes, almost always affected by the noble rot fungus.
Trockenbeerenauslese ('shrivelled selected berries') Intensely sweet wines made from individually picked grapes shrivelled by noble rot.
Eiswein ('ice wine') Made from frozen grapes picked in winter.

essentials REGULATIONS OUTSIDE EUROPE

In the United States, South America, Australia, New Zealand and South Africa, regulations govern statements about the place of origin and the grape varieties used. They help to ensure that the labelling is honest, but don't generally tell you anything about quality. Australia, however, has introduced Outstanding and Superior gradings for its top vineyards. Canada has a quality-based system; look for the letters VQA on the label.

Recommended wines

Throughout this part of the book I have put together selections of wines to try, to help you to discover the flavours of the wine regions of the world through the wines of good producers. The producers' names are shown in **bold**. You won't find all of these wines in your local shops, but mail-order and Internet wine merchants serve wine drinkers well. Also, any other wines you come across from producers I have recommended are worth trying.

The wines are listed in ascending price order and range from inexpensive ones for everyday drinking to high-priced examples for special occasions. I've given a rough indication of the prices of the wines by splitting them into five price bands:

1 Inexpensive   2 Mid-priced   3 Moderately expensive
4 Expensive   5 Very expensive

See page 2 for more information on price bands.

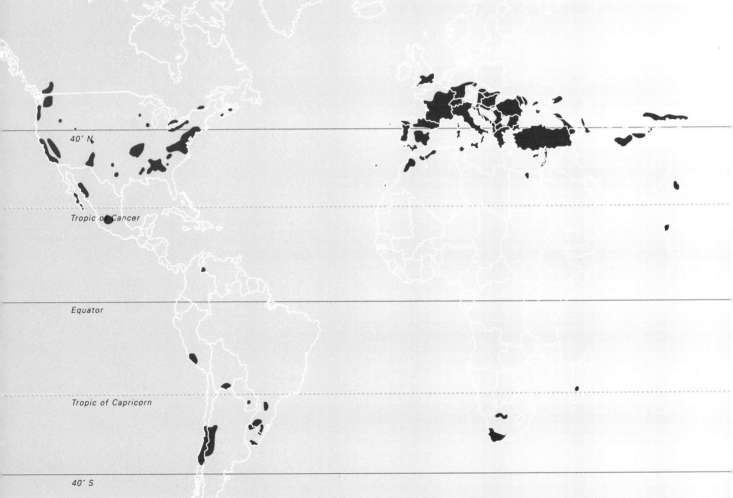

40° N

Tropic of Cancer

Equator

Tropic of Capricorn

40° S

Part III

The World of Wine

Once the only important places on the wine map of the world were European nations with long traditions of winemaking. Then, in the late 1970s, came the challenge from the so-called New World countries with their innovative ideas and bright, fresh, modern interpretations of the classic wines of Europe. California and Australia led the way and were joined by New Zealand and, more recently, Chile, Argentina and South Africa. But New World and Old World are attitudes of mind as well as places, and tradition and innovation now go hand in hand throughout the world of wine.

Vineyards have been established right around the globe, but almost entirely between 30° and 50°N and 30° and 40°S – the regions closer to the poles are too cold for vines, while those closer to the equator are mostly too hot to produce grapes suitable for winemaking.

France

Ah, France. Say the words 'French wine' and everybody's got a response: it's the best; the worst; too expensive; cheap plonk… whatever you think about France, the opposite is probably just as true. But nobody can deny that France is at the very heart of the world of wine.

What thrills me is the range of flavours I can find here. For a start, so many international wine styles have their origin in France. The worldwide vogue for Cabernet Sauvignon sprang from the cedary, blackcurranty flavours of red Bordeaux. Burgundy inspired the worldwide love of Chardonnay and Pinot Noir. Champagne has spawned a thousand sparkling imitators across the globe.

But the influence of the New World is being felt here as much as anywhere, and flavours have become softer and richer than they used to be. All the same, you should still expect French wines to be less obviously fruity than their New World counterparts. More subtle, in some cases; more austere in others.

Bear in mind, too, that France's reputation as a producer of great wines is based on the very top layer of quality. Below that things have always been more mixed. And if you go for the very cheapest French wines – well, frankly, you could be getting better value and better flavours in a dozen other countries.

essentials
FRENCH CLASSIFICATIONS

France, like all European Union countries, has a tiered classification system. The higher the grade, the stricter the rules covering place of origin, grape variety, method of growing and method of making. But don't ever mistake the Appellation Contrôlée classification for a guarantee of quality: it's not. Instead it's a guarantee that the wine comes from the region stated on the label, and was made in accordance with the law – just that and no more.

Appellation d'Origine Contrôlée (AC or AOC) The top grade of French wine applies stringent rules. Producers may only grow certain grape varieties in each area, and yields per hectare are regulated.

Vin Délimité de Qualité Supérieure (VDQS) A sort of junior AC. It accounts for just one per cent of French wine.

Vin de pays Relatively loosely regulated regions producing 'country wines' that are supposed to have the character of their region. Innovative winemakers love this category, because it allows them to do pretty well what they like.

Vin de table The most basic wine. The label won't state the region, and much is blended from all over France. It's seldom a good buy: stick to vin de pays instead.

🍷 Wine terms │ **Château**

Most wines in Bordeaux are called Château something-or-other. It may sound tremendously grand, and some châteaux are very grand indeed, but in Bordeaux it is simply the name given to a single estate, the size of which can vary from very large to just a hectare or two. A château is a brand name, in a sense: the wine varies from year to year according to the weather, but its basic style is always there.

PICTURE *Perfect harvest conditions at Château Palmer, one of the most attractive in Bordeaux.*

Bordeaux

If there is one single wine that for generations has carried the reputation of France, it is red Bordeaux. It is a benchmark wine throughout the world, and the origin of the intense, blackcurranty style of red, but there's one thing I want to make clear. Don't assume that because Château Margaux makes spectacularly wonderful wine, then the word Bordeaux on the label automatically equals prestige and quality. It doesn't. The wines of this region reach the heights, but they also plumb the depths of quality. The worst red Bordeaux is just dire, and it's not even cheap.

When I talk about the flavours of red Bordeaux I mean good to very good wines. Those flavours are, at their best, a complex blend of blackcurrants and plums, cedarwood and cigar boxes, with perhaps a touch of violets, perhaps a touch of roast coffee beans. They come especially from the Cabernet Sauvignon grape, which is always blended here, usually with both Merlot and Cabernet Franc. Wines with a lot of Merlot in the blend taste softer and more generously fruity.

This level of quality costs a lot of money, but, in general, these are the only red Bordeaux worth buying. The finest estates here produce sublime wine, of immense complexity and fascination. If you can afford these treasures, good for you. Top red Bordeaux is out of reach of most of us except for the most special of special occasions.

Bordeaux also makes a fair bit of white wine, which can be sweet or dry. The most famous golden, sweet whites are those of Sauternes and its neighbour, Barsac, and there are various lesser regions that produce lighter versions of this style. Oddly (considering my strictures on the lesser red wines) these wines can be rather good buys.

Dry whites also come up with the goods at the cheaper end. Basic white Bordeaux is a good bet these days. At the very least it will be fresh and clean and have some attractive grassy fruit. These wines are simple, less pungent versions of the green, tangy style typified by New Zealand Sauvignon Blanc. The same grape variety grows here, too, and is sometimes blended with Sémillon, sometimes not. At the top end, creamy, nectariny dry whites from Pessac-Léognan can be some of the best in France.

Bordeaux Clairet is, depending on your point of view, a dark rosé or a very light red wine. Either way, it's a good-value dry wine with a refreshing taste of summer fruits.

Do regions matter?

The simple answer is yes. The basic distinction is between those regions that grow a lot of Cabernet Sauvignon (the Médoc, Haut-Médoc, Pessac-Léognan and Graves) and those that specialise in Merlot (St-Émilion and Pomerol). Cabernet Sauvignon-based wines have more tannin and a more austere flavour than the Merlot-based wines, especially when young.

On the map you'll see some less illustrious regions marked, like Côtes de Castillon, Côtes de Bourg, Côtes de Blaye and Fronsac. All these places make red wine, and they're often good spots to look if you want simpler flavours and

  Wine terms | **Claret**

For 300 years, from 1152 to 1453, Bordeaux owed allegiance to the English crown. No wonder that England, and later on, the English-speaking world, developed such a taste for the wine. Some of it was known as **clairet** because of its light style compared to the gutsier wines of Spain or Portugal; and the name became Anglicised to **claret**. The name claret is still widely used in Britain, and applies to all red Bordeaux, while *clairet* is now the name for rosé-style wines from this region.

RIGHT *Château Angélus from St-Émilion is one of Bordeaux's most highly regarded red wines.*

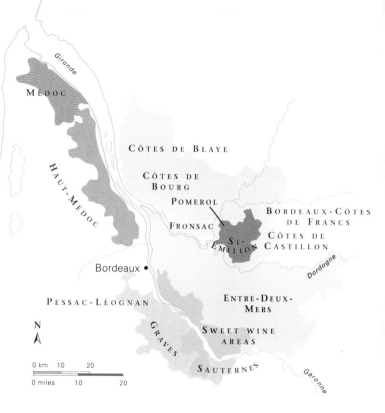

MÉDOC

Gironde

CÔTES DE BLAYE

CÔTES DE BOURG

HAUT-MÉDOC

POMEROL

FRONSAC

BORDEAUX-CÔTES DE FRANCS

ST-ÉMILION

CÔTES DE CASTILLON

Dordogne

Bordeaux •

PESSAC-LÉOGNAN

ENTRE-DEUX-MERS

N

GRAVES

SWEET WINE AREAS

SAUTERNES

Garonne

0 km 10 20
0 miles 10 20

BORDEAUX HIERARCHIES

Bordeaux has three tiers of AC wines. The basic AC Bordeaux covers the whole region, which is subdivided into districts with their own appellations. Within these are a few small appellations based around **communes** with exceptionally good land.

But the château is the crucial indicator of the quality of the wine, and top districts have lists of top performers, known as **crus classés** or classed growths. The most famous classification (made in 1855) rates the top 61 red wine châteaux on the Left Bank of the Gironde from First Growth (Premier Cru) to Fifth (Cinquième Cru). A further 300 or so in this area hold the rank of Cru Bourgeois. Sauternes gives the top award of First Great Growth (Premier Grand Cru) followed by First and Second Growths. Graves simply picks out Crus Classés; St-Émilion has Premiers Grands Crus followed by Grands Crus.

Even the most flexible of these systems doesn't keep pace with changes in quality year by year, so it's rather refreshing that Pomerol doesn't bother with *crus* at all.

Quick guide | Bordeaux

Location Bordeaux is situated on the Atlantic coast in the South-West of France.

Grapes Intense, blackcurranty reds are made from blends of varying proportions of Cabernet Sauvignon, Merlot and Cabernet Franc, with smaller amounts of Petit Verdot and Malbec. Sémillon and Sauvignon Blanc are the main white grapes for both dry and sweet wines.

Cabernet-dominated communes Listrac, Margaux, Moulis, Pauillac, St-Estèphe, St-Julien (all in the Haut-Médoc); Graves, Pessac-Léognan.

Merlot-dominated communes Pomerol, St-Émilion.

Local jargon *Left Bank, Right Bank* – reds from the Médoc, Haut-Médoc, Graves and Pessac-Léognan, the appellations on the left bank of the Gironde, are colloquially known as Left Bank wines; those from St-Émilion, Pomerol and other regions on the river's right bank are called Right Bank wines. Left Bank wines are Cabernet-dominated; Right Bank wines major on Merlot. *Grand Vin* – this means that the bottle contains the main wine of a château; it doesn't refer to the quality of the wine. *Second wine* – some châteaux produce a second wine from younger vines, or lesser parts of the vineyard than the Grand Vin. They can be a good buy. *Petit château* – a general term for the mass of unclassified châteaux in Bordeaux. Some are good, but many produce dross.

Vintages to look for 1998, 1996, 1995, 1990, 1989, 1988, 1986, 1985.

Vintages to avoid 1992, 1991, 1987; also 1994 and 1993 for Sauternes.

Fifteen to try
Red
- **Château la Prade** Bordeaux-Côtes de Francs ②
- **Château Annereaux** Lalande-de-Pomerol ③
- **Château la Tour-de-By** Médoc ③
- **Château Canon-de-Brem** Canon-Fronsac ③
- **Château Roc de Cambes** Côtes de Bourg ④
- **Château d'Angludet** Margaux ④
- **Château Chauvin** St-Émilion ④
- **Château Poujeaux** Moulis ④
- **Château Léoville-Barton** St-Julien ⑤
Dry white
- **Château Bonnet** Bordeaux Blanc ②
- **Château Carsin** Premières Côtes de Bordeaux ②
- **Château Reynon** Vieilles Vignes Bordeaux Sec ②
- **Château Haut Bertinerie** Premières Côtes de Blaye ②
Sweet white
- **Château Loubens** Ste-Croix-du-Mont ④
- **Château Lafaurie-Peyraguey** Sauternes ⑤

lower prices. Flavours are at best juicier and fruitier than those of top wines, but at worst leaner and more austere, and which you get depends as much on the producer as the region. If somebody points you towards a good one, try it. Lalande-de-Pomerol produces some goodies in the Pomerol mould of rich, plummy fruit, and since Pomerol is rare and expensive they make a useful substitute; St-Georges-St-Émilion and Puisseguin-St-Émilion make simpler versions of St-Émilion, but there's so much basic St-Émilion about that it's harder to see a need for these.

The very best dry white Bordeaux comes from Pessac-Léognan and Graves. Simpler wines come from Entre-Deux-Mers or may just be labelled Bordeaux Blanc.

Sauternes and Barsac are the top sweet wine areas, but others, including Loupiac, Cérons and Ste-Croix-du-Mont, have some pretty good wines. Curiously, Monbazillac, the region that comes closest to Sauternes in style, is actually just outside the borders of Bordeaux.

Do vintages matter?

Vintages matter more in Bordeaux than in most places. The weather here can be blissfully warm and sunny one year, and cool and wet the next, so the wines can vary from intense and deep-fruited to lean and underripe. See the Quick Guide on page 79. All good red Bordeaux needs to age for a few years, but some vintages mature faster than others.

The simplest whites are less susceptible to vintage variation, and in any case should be drunk young. With top whites, take care with the vintage, and give them some age. Vintages matter terrifically with Sauternes because the noble rot fungus, which gives the wines their sweetness and character, can't be relied upon to show up every year.

When do I drink them?

If you're going to open a really good bottle of red Bordeaux, then it's an event. There's an air of formality about good Bordeaux that demands respect. Keep it for when you've got time to appreciate it and cook something that will flatter the wine (roast lamb, just cooked pink, is ideal).

Sauternes is just as special. Do what the Bordelais do, and drink it with Roquefort cheese. Believe me, the combination is sublime. The simple whites, however, have no social pretensions at all: take them on a picnic if you want, or drink them out of a tumbler. They won't mind.

Can I afford them?

Look, you've got to live a little. Once in your life fork out for a top bottle of red. Treat it properly and it shouldn't disappoint. Good whites, dry and sweet, are expensive too, but the everyday whites are excellent value. I think you will have gathered by now what I think about most of the everyday reds – search out Bordeaux Clairet instead.

Burgundy

Burgundy, like Bordeaux, is a classic region of France. The French name for the region, and the one you'll see on the label, is Bourgogne. It's home to three famous grape varieties, which make three benchmark styles of wine: silky, strawberryish Pinot Noir, intense, nutty Chardonnay, and juicy, fruity Gamay, the grape of Beaujolais.

Top Chardonnays and Pinot Noirs fetch millionaire prices, and are available in tiny quantities. Beaujolais is far less serious, and even at its best has no such aspirations. The first two have been imitated with great success elsewhere in the world, using the same grape varieties. Beaujolais has acted more as an inspiration – for juicy, fruity reds from a whole host of different grapes.

Pinot Noir is the most fascinating grape of all, the hardest to grow and the trickiest to vinify. Whereas Cabernet Sauvignon is robust and easy-going and seems to taste reliably Cabernet-like almost no matter what you do

Vineyard location is critical in the cool Burgundian climate. A few minutes' extra exposure to the warming rays of the sun each day can make the difference between a good vineyard and a great one.

Wine terms | Growers and négociants

In Burgundy wine may be bottled and sold by the **grower** or by a **négociant** (merchant) who buys up grapes and wines from a number of growers to sell under his own name. In the past the received wisdom was that growers' wines were better and more characterful than négociants'; generally that's still the case, but now there are a number of excellent négociants producing quite large quantities of classy wine. It's no longer possible to say that one is always better than the other, but I'd still favour the grower.

to it, Pinot Noir is light and subtle and will, at the least provocation, lose its freshness or its perfume or its ineffable silky quality. It takes a very good winemaker and a very good vine grower to make good Pinot Noir.

To get a picture of red Burgundy you have to add to the truculent nature of the grape the complexities of vineyard ownership in Burgundy. While Bordeaux is composed of large estates with clear boundaries, a Burgundian estate consists of tiny parcels of vines in perhaps 20 different vineyards. Likewise, each vineyard in Burgundy is divided between many different owners. It's due to the way the French inheritance laws work. Each estate will make a different wine from each block of vines. Each wine will have a different name, and (in theory) a different character.

essentials
BURGUNDY CLASSIFICATIONS

Generic appellations As well as basic Bourgogne Rouge and Bourgogne Blanc, which can come from anywhere in the region, there are two undistinguished red styles that are seen relatively little these days, Bourgogne Grand Ordinaire and Bourgogne Passe-Tout-Grains. The Aligoté grape has its own appellation: Bourgogne Aligoté.

Regional appellations For example, Côte de Nuits-Villages, or Côte Chalonnaise. There is no actual Côte d'Or appellation: the Côte d'Or is divided into the Côte de Nuits and the Côte de Beaune.

Village appellations Most villages in the Côte d'Or have their own appellation, such as Gevrey-Chambertin, and so do some in the other regions, notably Beaujolais.

Premier Cru this term means First Growth but applies to the second-best vineyards. The vineyard name will appear on the label – though Burgundy also has some vineyards which are not Premier Cru that may also appear by name on the label. Either way, a vineyard name is a good sign.

Grand Cru These are the very best vineyards. They are appellations contrôlées in their own right, so may dispense with the name of their village on the label. Le Chambertin, for example, is a Grand Cru wine from the vineyard of Le Chambertin in the village of Gevrey-Chambertin.

These facts alone make Burgundy far harder to grasp than Bordeaux. In Bordeaux the name of the vineyard and the name of the producer are identical and interchangeable; in Burgundy, you need to know the name of both the vineyard and the producer.

You might gather from this that Burgundy, both red and white, is a specialist wine and not one to buy carelessly. You'd be right. In Burgundy, more than anywhere else, it pays to seek knowledgeable advice. Buy from a bad producer and you'll wonder what all the fuss is about.

Chardonnay in Burgundy is easier to grow, easier to make and easier to buy than Pinot Noir. It's far more reliable, but it's in just as great demand, so prices are high. It comes in a number of styles. Chablis is as lean and minerally as Chardonnay gets, but ages to a nutty complexity after several years. In the Côte d'Or, the world-famous heart of the region, flavours range from the oatmeal and nuts of the simpler wines to the long-lived butter and cream of the very best. In the Côte Chalonnaise and the Mâconnais flavours get simpler again, more like melon and apple. Chardonnay is also the grape of most sparkling Crémant de Bourgogne, a soft, honeyish fizz.

There's also a little lean, lemony wine made from Aligoté, a white grape grown in small quantities but to good effect. It rarely attains the weight of a really good Chardonnay, and is usually best drunk young.

And Beaujolais? It's a region devoted to one red grape, Gamay, and offers several variations on a basic light and bright, juicy, fruity taste. Beaujolais-Villages has the juiciest flavours. Simple Beaujolais and Beaujolais Nouveau can be as good but often lack fruit. Drink them all young. A Beaujolais from one of the ten top villages, known as the Beaujolais *crus*, should have more character and depth. The most notable *crus* are light Chiroubles, fragrant Fleurie and heavier wines from Morgon and Moulin-à-Vent.

Do regions matter?

Absolutely. If you want Chardonnay, it is leaner and crisper in Chablis, fuller and more complex on the Côte d'Or, broader and simpler in the Côte Chalonnaise, light and fairly crisp in the Mâconnais. If you want Pinot Noir, the finest wines come from the Côte d'Or; wines from the Côte Chalonnaise are earthier. Within the Côte d'Or each village has its own style, and within each village there is a hierarchy of vineyards. If you want Gamay you have the choice between juicy, simple Beaujolais, the *cru* wines, which are more serious and will often age for a few years, or the mostly unexciting reds of the Mâconnais.

Do vintages matter?

Yes, but the name of the producer matters more. See the Quick Guide, right.

When do I drink them?

The best Burgundies are indulgent, hedonistic wines and I drink them with indulgent, hedonistic friends. I wouldn't waste them on people who take themselves too seriously. When I'm drinking good Bordeaux I feel I ought to be wearing a tie and sitting up straight. Give me a glass of good Burgundy and I'll take off my jacket and relax. Give me a good Beaujolais and I'll kick off my shoes as well.

Can I afford them?

There's no getting around the fact that good Burgundy is expensive. But if you're clever (and get clever advice) you can find some wines that are remarkably good value. The trick for reds is to go for a good producer based in the Côte d'Or, but buy the the simpler wines, like Bourgogne Rouge or Chorey-lès-Beaune. The price will be far less than that of grander appellations. You won't get the full weight and complexity, but you'll get the elegance and silkiness. The same goes for Chardonnay. However, when it comes to basic white Burgundy from the Côte Chalonnaise and the Mâconnais, I would say that in many cases you will be better off with an Australian or Chilean Chardonnay.

As for Beaujolais: yes, you can afford it. It's probably overpriced for what has always been an everyday country wine, but it's delicious when it's good.

Quick guide | Burgundy

Location Burgundy's vineyards form a narrow belt of land stretching north-south through eastern France.

Grapes Pinot Noir for silky, strawberryish reds; Gamay for juicy, fruity ones. Chardonnay makes intense, nutty whites but can also be bone dry and neutral in Chablis; Aligoté is crisp and lemony.

Local jargon *Climat* – an individual vineyard site. *Clos* – a walled vineyard. *Côte* – a hillside. *Domaine* – an estate. *Négociant* – a merchant.

Vintages to look for 1999, 1998, 1997, 1996, 1995, 1993, 1990, 1989, 1988.

Vintages to avoid (red) 1994, 1992.

Ten to try
Red
• **Georges Duboeuf** Fleurie la Madone (Beaujolais *cru*) ②
• **Domaine Michel Lafarge** Bourgogne Rouge ③
• **Tollot-Beaut** Chorey-lès-Beaune ③
• **Chevillon** Nuits-St-Georges ④
• **Jadot** Beaune Teurons ④
White
• **Cave de Buxy** Montagny 1er cru ②
• **Vincent** St-Véran Château de Fuissé ②
• **Domaine Defaix** Chablis ③
• **Sauzet** Bourgogne Blanc ④
• **Louis Carillon** Puligny-Montrachet ⑤

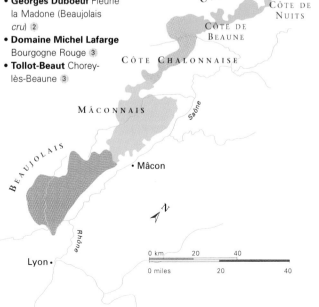

Quick guide | Champagne

Location The most northerly major wine region in France, situated north-east of Paris.

Grapes Chardonnay gives elegance to Champagne; Pinot Noir gives weight; and Pinot Meunier gives softness. Most Champagnes are a blend of all three grape varieties.

Local jargon *nv* – a commonly used abbreviation for non-vintage (see box, opposite). *Grand Cru* – wine made entirely from grapes from the region's very best vineyards. *Premier Cru* – wine made entirely from grapes from vineyards just one notch down from Grand Cru. *Blanc de Blancs* – white wine made entirely from white grapes: Chardonnay, in other words. Blanc de Blancs Champagne should be fresh, creamy and bright. *Blanc de Noirs* – white wine made entirely from the region's black grapes, Pinot Noir and Pinot Meunier. Blanc de Noirs Champagne should be weightier than other styles.

Vintages to look for 1996, 1993, 1990, 1989, 1988.

Vintages to avoid 1994, 1992 and 1991 aren't bad, but choose something else if you can.

Ten to try
All these producers make good vintage Champagne as well as non-vintage (nv), but Billecart-Salmon's is particularly reliable and good value.
- **Lanson** nv ④
- **Moët et Chandon** nv ⑤
- **Louis Roederer** nv ⑤
- **Bollinger** nv ⑤
- **Veuve Clicquot** nv ⑤
- **Charles Heidsieck** nv ⑤
- **Pol Roger** nv ⑤
- **Henriot** nv ⑤
- **Billecart-Salmon** Cuveé N F Billecart vintage ⑤
- **Krug** nv ⑤

ABOVE *Well-known Champagnes are still often referred to as Grandes Marques, although the term is officially defunct. It was never a guarantee of quality, only of fame.* RIGHT *Champagne is one of the coldest wine-producing regions in the world.*

Champagne

Champagne is the world's benchmark sparkling wine. Even when Australian or Californian producers set out to make a slightly different style, Champagne is the point they start from, and they often use the same grapes – Chardonnay, Pinot Noir and Pinot Meunier. It's one of the most famous wines in the world, and because most is sold under big brand names it's one of the simplest to buy.

The key to the flavour of good Champagne is that it doesn't taste obviously fruity. Instead it mingles fruit with biscuits or fresh bread or nuts or even chocolate, and it softens and mellows with age to a glorious nutty complexity. At least, that's the ideal. The method of production, which I've outlined on page 28, is what gives Champagne this flavour – as well as the bubbles.

Not all Champagne measures up; some can be lean and green and mean. Partly it depends on the weather – cold wet summers produce unripe-tasting Champagne – but mostly it depends on the producer. Happily most big names are reliably good these days.

Champagne can benefit from bottle age, even after you've bought it. If you tuck a non-vintage Champagne away in a cupboard for six months it will gain extra roundness; and vintage Champagne isn't at its best until at least a decade after the vintage.

Do regions matter?

Only if you live there and have to find your way around.

Do vintages matter?

Most Champagne is non-vintage, which means that it is a blend of several vintages. All houses keep stocks of older vintages so that they can blend to a consistent style year by year. Vintage Champagne, in which the vintage obviously does matter, is (in theory) only produced in the best years. You'll pay extra for vintage wines, and what you get for your money should be extra depth, extra character, extra weight – extra everything. Yet vintage Champagnes are not just bigger versions of non-vintage. There should

CHAMPAGNE STYLES

Champagne comes in three tiers of quality and richness:

Non-vintage is the lightest. It's a blend of wines from several years, and can be drunk as soon as you buy it, though will benefit from a further six months' aging.

Vintage is only made in good years. It should be richer and more flavoursome than non-vintage, but needs to mature for a decade.

De luxe cuvées are mostly, but not all, vintage. They are the very top wines, sold in fancy bottles for huge prices. Dom Pérignon is an example. They should live for decades.

Rosé Champagne is weightier than white, with a more strawberryish, toasty flavour. There are also levels of sweetness, though most Champagne is sold as **brut** (dry). **Ultra brut** or **brut zéro** is even drier, while **extra dry** is, bizarrely, slightly less dry. **Sec** is off-dry, **demi-sec** (sometimes labelled **rich**) is medium sweet.

be extra complexity, too, and the character of the year should show through. See the Quick Guide, opposite.

When do I drink it?

Any time, any place, anywhere. It's great to drink on the beach, in the bath, for breakfast, at smart parties – anywhere. Vintage Champagne is a more serious sort of wine than non-vintage and you probably ought to pay proper attention to it. Trouble is, Champagne always makes me feel so frivolous and feckless that I forget to treat it with any reverence at all. But vintage Champagne goes well with food and non-vintage is the better choice for parties, if that's any help.

Can I afford it?

When you really want it, of course you can. Just give up something else. The cheapest Champagne can be pretty grim, but lots of good merchants have an excellent own-label Champagne at well below the big-brand prices.

The Rhône Valley

If you want spicy, warm-hearted wines of remarkable depth and complexity, this is where you come. At least, this is where you come in France, because the Rhône Valley is the French home of the Syrah grape, which produces rich flavours of herbs and smoke. The grape's other home is Australia, where it is known as Shiraz, so if you want to get a full picture of the grape's flavours, compare a good Rhône red with a softer, more obviously fruity Barossa Valley Shiraz. It's the difference between Old World and New World styles encapsulated in a single grape variety.

There's a division in the Rhône, however, between North and South. On the map it's shaped a bit like an upturned funnel: narrow at the top, then abruptly widening at the base. Well, the narrow bit is the North, where Syrah is the only red grape planted. Where it widens is the South, and a whole range of grapes is planted here – 13 of them are allowed for the various appellations. Wines from the South don't have the minerally, smoky austerity of the northern wines. Instead they're broader and more generous – mostly because the soft, juicy Grenache grape is part of the blend. And of course there's far more wine made in the South. That has two effects for us: first, prices are generally higher in the North. Secondly, quality is more variable in the South.

That's the red wines. When it comes to whites, the Rhône starts springing surprises. With the Viognier grape it produces some of the most aromatic whites in the world, with a flavour of apricots mingled with spring flowers and hopefully a whiff of spice. Viognier's traditional home is in a couple of tiny, high-priced appellations in the northern Rhône, Condrieu and Château-Grillet.

The good news is that growers in the southern Rhône have caught on to the fact that we all love Viognier, or

would if we could afford it, and they're busy planting it, so some cheaper versions are appearing. They're not, I have to admit, quite as magical as Condrieu or Château-Grillet, but they do show the grape's astonishing flavours.

The other white grapes of the northern Rhône are Marsanne and Roussanne. This duo is responsible for the other dry whites of the North – white Hermitage, Crozes-Hermitage, St-Joseph and St-Péray – and they give a broad herby flavour that's quite unusual. The dry whites of the South vary according to the cocktail of grapes used, but if you think of them as having strong leafy and herby rather than fruity flavours, sometimes softened by honeysuckle, then you won't go far wrong.

The South has one more trick to pull yet. It's the Muscat grape, making golden, sweet wines that pack a head-reeling punch of crunchy, grapy flavours, laced with rose petals and orange spice, and yet manage to be elegant with it. These wines pack quite a punch of alcohol too,

Quick guide | The Rhône Valley

Location The Rhône Valley is in south-east France. The vineyards are split into two regions with separate identities: the steep slopes of the northern Rhône and the hot plains of the southern Rhône.

Grapes Syrah is the red grape of the North, making smoky, minerally wines; southern reds are made from a cocktail of grapes, including Syrah and juicy Grenache, for softer, broader flavours. All Rhône reds are variants of the spicy, warm-hearted style. Viognier is a highly aromatic white grape, while Marsanne and Roussanne deliver herby flavours. Muscat is used in the southern Rhône for fortified golden, sweet wines.

Syrah-dominated communes (all in the North) Cornas, Côte-Rôtie, Crozes-Hermitage, Hermitage, St-Joseph.

Appellations where reds are mostly blends (all in the South) Châteauneuf-du-Pape, Coteaux du Tricastin, Côtes du Lubéron, Côtes du Rhône, Côtes du Rhone-Villages, Côtes du Ventoux, Gigondas, Lirac, Vacqueyras.

Viognier communes Château-Grillet, Condrieu.

Vintages to look for (northern reds) 1999, 1998, 1997, 1996, 1995, 1991, 1990; (southern reds) 1999, 1998, 1995, 1994, 1990.

Vintages to avoid 1993 for northern reds.

Ten to try
Red
- **Chapoutier** Côtes du Rhône Belleruche ②
- **Graillot** Crozes-Hermitage ②
- **Domaine Santa Duc** Gigondas Cuvée Tradition ②
- **Cuilleron** St-Joseph ③
- **Domaine du Vieux Télégraphe** Châteauneuf-du-Pape ③
- **Verset** Cornas ④
White
- **Guigal** Côtes du Rhône ②
- **Gaillard** Côtes du Rhône Viognier ③
- **Perret** Condrieu Coteau de Chéry ⑤
Sweet white
- **Domaine de Durban** Muscat de Beaumes-de-Venise ③

The hill at Hermitage is the most famous of the northern Rhône's steep valley sides. Further south the valley floor broadens to an open plain.

because they're fortified with grape spirit. Muscat de Beaumes de Venise is the most famous and the best, but if you'll permit me to venture beyond the confines of the Rhône for a moment, I'll introduce you to some others scattered around the South of France – Muscat de Frontignan, Muscat de Mireval, Muscat de Rivesaltes and Muscat de St-Jean-de-Minervois.

Do regions matter?

There are differences between North and the South, but the reds are basically all spicy and warm-hearted and the whites, with the exception of aromatic Viognier, are intriguingly herb-scented wherever they come from.

Do vintages matter?

People talk about a given vintage being better in the North than in the South, or vice versa. But don't get too hung up on Rhône vintages – they're rarely bad. See the Quick Guide on page 87.

When do I drink them?

It's a question of mood, as well as food. The reds are cold-weather wines; they're far too robust for a summer's day. You can almost feel warmth emanating from the bottle. They're happiest with strongly flavoured food: a rich casserole, a peppered steak or a slice of saucisson.

Viognier will go with some foods, but it's so unexpected in flavour that you might enjoy it best on its own. As for the other dry whites, well, drink them for the sake of trying a flavour you won't find elsewhere. They're quite versatile partners for food. You can drink the sweet fortified Muscats as apéritifs – that's what the French do – but they're also a rare match for chocolaty puddings.

Can I afford them?

The top wines, like top wines everywhere, are expensive and rising. Hermitage and Côte-Rôtie in the North and Châteauneuf-du-Pape in the South are the priciest appellations for reds. Viognier from Condrieu and Château-Grillet is astronomically expensive. But there are lots of tasty wines at the middle and lower end which are very affordable and very good value.

The South isn't uniform in quality – it's too big for that – and the Côtes du Rhône appellation, which covers the whole region, includes everything from rich, concentrated wines to thin, dilute ones. The answer is partly to shun the very lowest priced examples; they will be the worst, and hardly worth drinking. Pay more for a single-domaine wine from a serious producer, and you'll get far better value for your money.

The Loire Valley

The Loire Valley is the place for classically French flavours that aren't much imitated elsewhere in the world. Both whites and reds are popular in Paris restaurants, where they are the lunchtime wines of choice. And why not? They're great with food and quality is on a roll in the wake of some excellent vintages in the 1990s.

The white wines are the easiest to find outside France. The best are green and tangy: think pungency; think minerally acidity. In fact the Loire produces two versions of this style, one made from Sauvignon Blanc, the grape New Zealand does with a great big blast of fruit; and one made from Chenin Blanc, which nobody and nowhere else in the world does so well.

Both grapes have a flavour that can be pretty alarming the first time you encounter it, but the refreshing zestiness of Sauvignon Blanc is more immediately likeable. Chenin

 Wine terms | **Know your Pouillys**

Pouilly-Fumé is the Loire's famous crisp, refreshing wine made from Sauvignon Blanc. It has a slight smoky edge that earns it the 'Fumé' tag. Don't confuse this with **Pouilly-sur-Loire**, an unmemorable wine made in the same area from a grape called Chasselas. And don't mix it up with **Pouilly-Fuissé, Pouilly-Loché** or **Pouilly-Vinzelles**. These are rich, buttery Chardonnay wines and they come from Burgundy.

Quick guide | The Loire Valley

Location A large region stretching the length of the River Loire from central France to the west coast.

Grapes Sauvignon Blanc and Chenin Blanc make green, tangy whites; Melon de Bourgogne is the neutral grape of Muscadet. Cabernet Franc and Pinot Noir make generally light versions of intense, blackcurranty reds; Gamay is simple and light.

Sauvignon Blanc appellations Menetou-Salon, Quincy, Reuilly, Pouilly-Fumé, Sancerre.

Chenin Blanc appellations Anjou Blanc, Montlouis, Saumur Blanc, Savennières, Vouvray.

Sweet Chenin Blanc appellations Bonnezeaux, Coteaux de l'Aubance, Coteaux du Layon, Montlouis, Quarts de Chaume, Vouvray.

Local jargon *Sec* – dry. *Moelleux* – sweet. *Liquoreux* – very sweet. *Sur lie* – aged on lees. *Crémant* – traditional-method fizz. *Mousseux* – sparkling.

① Muscadet
② Anjou-Saumur
③ Touraine
④ Sancerre and Pouilly-Fumé

Vintages to look for 1998 (not sweet wines), 1997, 1996, 1995, 1990, 1989.

Ten to try
Red
- **Château de Fesles** Anjou Rouge Vieilles Vignes ②
- **Domaine Filliatreau** Saumur-Champigny ②
Dry white
- **Domaine Richou** Anjou Blanc ①
- **Sauvion & Fils** Muscadet de Sèvre-et-Maine Sur Lie ①
- **Domaine des Aubuisières** Vouvray ②
- **Crochet** Sancerre ②
- **Château de Tracy** Pouilly-Fumé ③
Sweet white
- **Baumard** Quarts de Chaume ⑤
- **Huet** Vouvray Clos du Bourg Moelleux ⑤
Sparkling white
- **Langlois-Château** Crémant de Loire ③

ABOVE *Domaine des Aubuisières produces excellent Vouvray in styles from dry to sweet.* LEFT *Sauvignon is the main grape of the hilltop town of Sancerre.*

Blanc takes a bit more getting to know, but its steely, appley fruit, high acidity and minerally streak mature, in the best examples, to a wonderful richness of honey and quince. The more serious wines from Vouvray and Savennières need bottle age. Several years' bottle age at least. Saumur is lighter, and can be drunk young.

Chenin Blanc also makes splendid sweet wines from grapes affected by noble rot: look for Vouvray *moelleux*, Quarts de Chaume, Bonnezeaux and Coteaux du Layon. Tuck them away in a dark corner for a long time, because they really need bottle age – ten years or more from the vintage date – to turn their piercing sweetness and acidity to a marvellous, mellow, quince-and-honey richness.

There's a third major white wine in the Loire, which is Muscadet. The grape here is called Melon de Bourgogne, and as for flavour – well, it doesn't have much. It's about as neutral as white wine can get, which makes it all the more remarkable that there are several different Muscadet appellations with, in theory, slightly different styles. Never mind: all you really need to look for on the label are the words *sur lie*, which mean the wine was aged on the creamy, yeasty-tasting lees left over after fermentation – the lees being the dead yeasts. Aging it this way gives it a bit of life and creamy depth and makes all the difference between interesting neutrality and boring neutrality.

When we get to the Loire's reds, it's worth bearing in mind that these are wines very much in the French mould. Yes, they have plenty of fruit flavour, but it's not upfront fruit flavour in the New World style. They are grassy, redcurranty, raspberryish, even plummy, but they are far more restrained than anything an Australian or Californian winemaker would produce. And, while a few are quite weighty, most are decidedly lightweight compared to the average New World red.

So, do I like them? Oh yes! They're utterly delicious and wonderful value, and they're utterly wonderful with food. The major grape is Cabernet Franc. There's also a little Pinot Noir, which here is altogether more rustic than red Burgundy, without the sweet perfume or the silkiness.

Gamay here is pretty much like basic Beaujolais but, if it's from a decent producer, gutsier and better.

The Loire also produces fairly sharp sparkling wines made in the same way as Champagne. The whites have a more appley fruit than Champagne and there are a few strawberryish sparkling rosés, too. Ah, yes, rosé. The Loire lets itself down with sweetish still Anjou Rosé, which is seldom much fun. Cabernet d'Anjou is usually drier, tastier and more likely to please.

Do regions matter?

Different regions grow different grapes, so yes. Sancerre and Pouilly-Fumé in the east grow Sauvignon Blanc and Pinot Noir; Anjou and Touraine in the middle grow mostly Chenin Blanc and Cabernet Franc, though the best Touraine whites are Sauvignon Blanc; and the Pays Nantais in the west grows Melon for Muscadet.

Do vintages matter?

They do, and it's a complicated picture. Chenin Blanc and the red grapes do best in the warmest years; but if it's too warm the Sauvignon Blanc gets flabby. The great sweet wines are only made in the most favourable years. See the Quick Guide on page 89.

When do I drink them?

Chenin Blanc and the reds cry out for food – their balance, their subtlety are brilliant as part of a meal. The reds, in particular, are perfect for drinking in the summer, and they're good enough for quite grand dinner parties should you wish. Muscadet should only be considered if you have a plate of seafood in front of you – and in those circumstances there can be nothing better.

Can I afford them?

Chenin Blanc is great value; the reds are great value. Sancerre and Pouilly-Fumé are on the pricy side and other wines made from Sauvignon Blanc are cheaper. Muscadet is overpriced for its quality.

Alsace

When it comes to aromatic white wines, no region in the world can match Alsace. These wines all share a rich, dry spiciness, a fatness quite unlike anything from the rest of France, or anywhere else in the world.

Gewurztraminer is the spiciest, most fragrant grape of the lot – it's the benchmark for the aromatic white wine style – but even a grape like Pinot Blanc, which everywhere else makes a rather well-behaved, sober sort of wine, becomes lush in Alsace. Sylvaner, too, normally a light, dry and rather neutral individual, here has a touch of spice. Riesling, which in Australia is limy and toasty, and in Germany minerally and smoky and peachy, here is – yes, spicy. And Pinot Gris is second only to Gewurztraminer in its richness, though it tends to be smoky, earthy and honeyed rather than rose- and lychee-scented like the latter.

The exception to the rich, spicy rule is the tiny amount of dry Muscat made in Alsace, but it wins through with a heavenly floral, grapy aroma which, in its own way, is almost as intense as that of Gewurztraminer.

And these wines are all dry. That means they go well with food, particularly spicy foods, or foods that mix sweet and savoury flavours.

There are sweet whites, too. The richest are made from nobly rotten grapes, but they're rare and expensive. The locals drink them with foie gras. There's also some light red, made from Pinot Noir, but it's generally little more than dark rosé – perfectly attractive, but not up to the quality of the whites.

 Wine terms | **Late harvest styles**

Grapes left to develop beyond the usual harvest time develop extra ripeness if bad weather holds off. Alsace wines made from these grapes are called **Vendange Tardive** (literally 'late harvest'), and they are full-bodied and alcoholic, ranging in sweetness from richly dry to dessert-sweet. Luscious sweet wines produced from the rarer grapes affected by **noble rot** are called **Sélection de Grains Nobles**. All these wines can age for ten years or even longer.

Quick guide | Alsace

Location In the North-East, on the German border.

Grapes The white grapes, in ascending order of spiciness and intensity, are: Sylvaner, Pinot Blanc, Riesling, Pinot Gris (sometimes called Tokay-Pinot Gris here), Muscat (floral rather than spicy) and Gewurztraminer. There's also Pinot Noir for light reds. Most wines are labelled by the grape name.

Local jargon *Grand Cru* – the official classification of the 50 top vineyards, which make wine of greater depth and interest. *Edelzwicker* – a lightweight blend of several grapes, generally not very thrilling. *Special reserve* – this and similar terms have no legal weight. Producers use them to distinguish one wine from another, but they are not a quality guarantee.

Vintages to look for 1998, 1997, 1995, 1990, 1989.

Vintages to avoid 1994 and 1991 weren't great.

Ten to try
White
- **Cave Co-opérative de Turckheim** Gewurztraminer ②
- **Josmeyer** Pinot Blanc Mise du Printemps ②
- **Albert Mann** Riesling ②
- **Ostertag** Sylvaner Vieilles Vignes ②

- **Cave de Pfaffenheim** Tokay-Pinot Gris ②
- **Schoffit** Gewurztraminer Cuvée Caroline ②
- **Rolly Gassmann** Muscat Moenchreben ③
- **Domaine Paul Blanck** Riesling Furstentum Vieilles Vignes ④
- **Zind-Humbrecht** Gewurztraminer Clos Windsbuhl ④
- **Domaine Weinbach** Tokay-Pinot Gris Cuvée Ste-Cathérine ④

Alsace villages seem to belong to an earlier age. This painted wrought iron sign advertising a wine producer's cellar is a typical feature of the narrow cobbled streets.

① Bergerac
② Cahors
③ Minervois
④ Corbières
⑤ Fitou
⑥ Bandol

Quick guide | Southern France

Location The vineyards are in three regions: the South-West, Languedoc-Roussillon and Provence.

Grapes In the South-West Cabernet Sauvignon, Cabernet Franc and Merlot are widely grown reds. Malbec has its moment of glory in Cahors. Tannat and Négrette are intriguing local varieties. Whites are often Sémillon and Sauvignon Blanc, but there is also a host of local grapes. Carignan is the traditional Languedoc-Roussillon red, but the better-quality Rhône reds, Grenache, Syrah, Mourvèdre and Cinsaut, are now being grown, too. International favourites, both white and red, are building their presence. Provence has the same red varieties plus Cabernet Sauvignon.

Ten to try
Red
- **Domaine Ste-Eulalie** Minervois ①
- **Domaine Gauby** Côtes du Roussillon ②
- **Château de Lastours** Corbières, Cuvée Simon Descamps ②
- **Mas Jullien** Coteaux du Languedoc, Les États d'Âme ②
- **Alquier** Faugères ②
- **Pech Redon** La Clape, Alicante ②
- **Château de Pibarnon** Bandol ③
Dry white
- **Domaine de la Baume** Vin de Pays d'Oc Sauvignon Blanc ①
- **Domaine de Cauhapé** Jurançon ②
Sweet white
- **Domaine Cazes** Muscat de Rivesaltes ③

Do regions matter?
No, all the wines are in the uniquely Alsatian style.

Do vintages matter?
The wonderful sweet wines are only made in the best years, and the reds need warm summers. But otherwise don't worry too much about vintages.

When do I drink them?
At any time. They're good restaurant choices because they'll go with a whole range of different foods around the table, and I've never met anyone who didn't like them. They're also unusual enough to impress at special occasions. Riesling is the best all-round food wine; Gewurztraminer and Pinot Gris are especially good with Chinese and other Asian foods. They are delicious on their own, too, and Muscat is a pure delight by itself.

Can I afford them?
Yes, certainly. They're never the cheapest wines in any shop, and the best ones are pretty pricy, but they can be bought with confidence at every level. Even the simplest wines will be good buys.

Southern France

This is where the excitement is in France right now, where the Old World meets the New. In the vin de pays regions, particularly Vin de Pays d'Oc, Australian and Australian-trained winemakers, lured by the tremendous potential of the vineyards, have been moving in to produce wines with typically New World upfront fruit, tempered with buttery new oak. Instead of the blends of traditional grape varieties used by the producers in the AC regions, they favour single-variety wines made from international grapes like Cabernet Sauvignon, Chardonnay and Sauvignon Blanc. They use Syrah as well, and some Viognier. Anything, in other words, with the potential for bags of quality and bags of flavour.

Do regions matter?

Yes, very much, because of the division between Old World and New World styles. In Bergerac and Côtes de Duras in the South-West you get red and white Bordeaux lookalikes. A little further from Bordeaux, you'll find wild, spicy, brawny and tannic reds in Cahors and Madiran.

In Languedoc-Roussillon the reds are spicy and often herb-scented, sometimes with a dry austerity as well. You'll find these flavours in the wines of Fitou, Minervois, Corbières, Faugères, Costières de Nîmes, St-Chinian, Coteaux du Languedoc and Côtes du Roussillon.

Provence, with the appellations of Bandol, Côtes de Provence, Coteaux d'Aix en Provence and Les Baux-de-Provence, makes both spicy, warm-hearted and intense, blackcurranty reds, plus a great many good rosés. The dominant grape often determines the style: Cinsaut makes the palest rosé; Syrah the tastiest rosé and red.

Vins de pays from Oc and elsewhere in the South should be juicier, more directly fruity interpretations of these red and rosé styles, and they also add white wines in the ripe, nutty and aromatic styles to the repertoire.

Traditional whites range from bone dry and neutral to those with a tang of wild herbs; Jurançon can be delightfully perfumed. Rosés are strawberryish and, again, have a whiff of herbs. Sparkling Blanquette de Limoux is sharp, refreshing and appley. There are some sweet, golden fortified Muscats, too, from Frontignan, Mireval, Rivesaltes and St-Jean-de-Minervois, and, next door to Bordeaux, the sweet, golden Sauternes-lookalikes of Monbazillac.

Do vintages matter?

Not really, but even here there are occasional aces.

When do I drink them?

Whenever you feel like it. The reds can be a bit assertive for hot weather, but the whites and rosés are perfect.

Can I afford them?

With the exception of a few cult wines, yes.

Under the gaze of the medieval Château d'Aiguilar old Carignan vines produce grapes for some of the most brooding red wines of Fitou.

This influence is also being felt in the traditional AC wines of the South-West, Languedoc-Roussillon and Provence. More and more producers are using improved techniques to get the best out of the many local grape varieties found throughout these regions, although the wines still taste resolutely Old World. Flavours in much of the South-West are influenced by Bordeaux. But as you get further from Bordeaux you'll find highly individual wines that are often robust and wildly herby, but which are increasingly showing the benefits of modern freshness. I love the dusty fruit of the traditional wines, when they're well-made; but I also love the sheer verve of the new vin de pays styles.

Italy

ITALY HAS ITS own grape varieties and its own way of doing things; and it's doing them better and better. Famous names like Soave, Valpolicella and Chianti are restoring the shine to their tarnished reputations, while the South is re-establishing itself with inexpensive wines, brimful of character, that every wine shop wants on its shelves.

Italy doesn't really make the sorts of wines that other countries do. Even when Italian producers use international grapes like Cabernet or Chardonnay or modern techniques like aging the wine in new oak, they give the wines a distinctive Italian twist.

So when do you opt for a bit of Italian style? When you're staring at a plate of food, that's when. The reds are full of sweet-sour cherryish fruit that sets your mouth watering, and the bone-dry, neutral whites are so well behaved they'll accompany even the most delicate dish. The whites make terrific apéritifs, but the reds need food.

Piedmont and the North-west

If you like powerful, scented reds that mature majestically, this is your region. Nebbiolo is the grape and Barolo, if you're feeling rich, is the summit of your ambition.

Quick guide | North-west Italy

Location Piedmont is the central and most significant region of north-west Italy.

Grapes Nebbiolo, Barbera and Dolcetto make reds in the mouthwatering sweet-sour style, with Nebbiolo being the weightiest and most perfumed. Spanna is a local nickname for Nebbiolo. Of the whites, Arneis is fairly aromatic; Moscato (the Italian name for Muscat) is very aromatic and used for sweet and sparkling wines; and Cortese is dry and crisp.

Nebbiolo-dominated regions Barbaresco, Barolo, Carema, Gattinara, Langhe, Nebbiolo d'Alba.

Barbera-dominated regions Barbera is grown everywhere in North-west Italy. DOCs include Barbera d'Alba and Barbera d'Asti.

Dolcetto-dominated regions DOCs include Dolcetto d'Acqui, Dolcetto d'Alba and Dolcetto d'Asti.

Local jargon *Bricco* – a prime hilltop vineyard. *Sorì* – a south-facing hillside vineyard (i.e. one that catches the best of the sun). *Spumante* – sparkling. *Riserva* – wine given extra aging before it goes on sale.

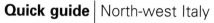

① Barolo and Barbaresco
② Asti

Vintages to look for 1999, 1998, 1997, 1996, 1995 (except Dolcetto), 1990.

Vintages to avoid 1994, 1993, 1992 and 1991 wines are generally poor value.

Ten to try
Red
- **Bava** Barbera d'Asti, Arbest 2
- **Albino Rocca** Dolcetto d'Alba 2
- **Elio Altare** Dolcetto d'Alba 2
- **Vajra** Langhe 3
- **Aldo Conterno** Barbera d'Alba, Conca Tre Pile 3
- **Ascheri** Barolo 3
- **Pio Cesare** Barbaresco 5
- **Domenico Clerico** Barolo, Ciabot Mentin Ginestra 5
White
- **Giuseppe Rivetti** Moscato d'Asti, La Spinetta 2
- **Giacosa** Roero Arneis 3

MAIN PICTURE *Nebbiolo gets its name from nebbia, the Italian word for fog, because it ripens late in the autumn when the hills are shrouded in mist.* LEFT *The very best and most expensive Barolos come from single vineyards, such as Aldo Conterno's Cicala.*

Barolo is a blockbuster of a red wine. Think of the scents of chocolate and cherries, of prunes and tobacco, of tar and of roses. Whirl them all together and you've got an idea of what Barolo tastes like. It used to be a wine that took years and years to age, but a new generation of modernising producers is making wines that are approachable far younger, and are far less tannic and forbidding. Other Nebbiolo wines – Barbaresco, Langhe, Nebbiolo d'Alba, Carema, Gattinara and Spanna – range from ripe and supple to rough and ready.

But Nebbiolo does not dominate the vineyards of the North-West. That role is left to Barbera, which crops up everywhere. High acidity and low tannin are its keynotes, together with flavours of slightly unripe plums and raisins; the best age well, but lots can be drunk young. The third main red grape is Dolcetto, which is juicier and fruitier than the other two, but still has that typical Italian tang, and often a good streak of tannin as well.

Whites are not a big deal round here, with the exception of deliciously grapy, sweet Asti and other sparkling wines made from the Muscat, or Moscato, grape. There's some aromatic Arneis and refreshing but overpriced Gavi, made from Cortese grapes, but it's reds that rule.

Do regions matter?
Yes, because styles vary. Barolo is the biggest, grandest Nebbiolo, followed by Barbaresco, followed by the others I mentioned above. Dolcetto d'Asti and Dolcetto d'Acqui tend to be lighter than Dolcetto d'Alba. Barbera d'Alba and Barbera d'Asti are the best Barbera wines.

Do vintages matter?
Yes, for the better reds. See the Quick Guide on page 95.

When do I drink them?
With food, in the case of the reds – and since the better reds are both expensive and very good, they do nicely for special occasions. Asti and the other sweet Moscato whites are perfect for summer drinking, or with rich desserts.

Can I afford them?
Top Barolo and Barbera are fantastically expensive. Go for a fairly simple Nebbiolo from a good producer – though it still won't be cheap. Barbera and Dolcetto are less costly; Asti is inexpensive and fun.

North-east Italy

This is white wine country. Not to the exclusion of reds, you understand, but let's start with the whites. They range in style from light and mountain-fresh up in the high Alto Adige to more substantial further south and east in the Veneto and Friuli. But bear in mind that Italian penchant for neutrality in white wines. Even with aromatic grapes like Sauvignon Blanc, you won't find anything like the pungency that you'll get from New Zealand. Pinot Grigio is generally light and crisp: quite different from Pinot Gris in Alsace. Sparkling Prosecco is fresh, bouncy and light.

A lot of wines round here are made from single grape varieties, and named by the grape, which makes it pretty easy to guess the flavour. Soave is the major exception. It's made from Garganega and Trebbiano grapes and is a typically Italian bone-dry, neutral white. Soave can be pretty classy, with surprising depth and ageability, but most are light and, so long as you buy Soave Classico from the heartland of the region, uncomplicated and agreeable.

Reds, including Valpolicella and Bardolino from the Veneto, are mostly light, but can have quite individual flavours. International grapes like Merlot are almost always much lighter than versions from other countries. However, if you see a Valpolicella labelled Recioto, it will be sweet, rich and probably wonderful. Buy it. (There's a white Recioto from Soave, too, which is just as good.) Amarone is like Recioto di Valpolicella, but dry: it's a fascinating, bitter-sour, heavyweight red.

Do regions matter?
Yes, hugely, since each region has its own style. Alto Adige makes the lightest wines; Trentino's are slightly fuller;

Grapes are partially dried on racks to concentrate their flavours for making the sweet Recioto and bitter Amarone styles of Valpolicella.

Friuli's the most intense. Valpolicella, Bardolino and Soave from the Veneto are the most famous. Quality here has been compromised by overproduction, but plenty of producers make the kind of wine that earned these regions their fame in the first place. Stick to wines labelled Classico and you are less likely to be disappointed.

Do vintages matter?
They do vary, but they're not worth worrying about unless you're buying Reciotos and Amarones or the most expensive whites. See the Quick Guide, right.

When do I drink them?
The whites are good as apéritifs, or as partners for light food. The light reds are for simple meals like pizza and pasta. Reciotos and Amarones are for feasts. The latter demand aging in bottle – up to ten years if you can wait.

Can I afford them?
Not all the wines are brilliant value. Friuli is expensive for the quality; Alto Adige relatively so. The Veneto, if you choose well, is not so expensive, especially for Valpolicella and Soave Classico.

Quick guide | North-east Italy

Location The Veneto and Friuli-Venezia Giulia are located around Venice. Further inland, Trentino-Alto Adige extends south into Italy from the Austrian Alps.

Grapes Garganega and Trebbiano are the grapes of Soave and other neutral whites. Red Corvina is the main grape of Valpolicella and Bardolino. Alto Adige has many local whites, plus light Traminer (Gewürztraminer). Tocai is a characterful white from Friuli. International white varieties include Pinot Bianco, Pinot Grigio, Chardonnay and Sauvignon Blanc. Reds include Merlot, Pinot Noir and Cabernet Sauvignon.

Local jargon *Classico* – the central heartland, and therefore the best part, of a region. *Recioto* – sweet Soave or Valpolicella made from semi-dried grapes. *Amarone* – Recioto, but fermented out to dryness. *Ripasso* – ordinary wine passed over the lees of Amarone to add a tangy

① Bardolino ③ Soave
② Valpolicella

flavour and increase the alcohol level.

Vintages to look for
(Amarone) 1999, 1997, 1995, 1993, 1990.

Vintages to avoid
(Amarone) 1992, 1991.

Ten to try
Red
• **Tedeschi** Valpolicella Classico Superiore ②
• **Zenato** Valpolicella Superiore Ripasso ②
• **Foradori** Teroldego Rotaliano ②
• **Villa Russiz** Collio Merlot Graf de la Tour ③
• **Allegrini** Amarone della Valpolicella Classico ④
White
• **Pieropan** Soave Classico Superiore ②
• **Jermann** Pinot Bianco ③
• **Mario Schiopetto** Collio Tocai Friulano ④
• **Anselmi** Recioto di Soave ④
Sparkling
• **Ferrari** Brut ④

Mario Schiopetto's intense Tocai Friulano is a highly scented white wine with a delicious flavour of citrus, pears and herbs.

Tuscany and central Italy

Chianti is far and away the most famous wine of this part of Italy – in fact it's probably the most famous wine of Italy, period. It's the essence of the sweet-sour cherryish style that dominates Italian reds, but there's a twist of tea leaves in there as well, and a whiff of violets, and a good backbone of tannin. And quality, you'll be glad to hear, is rising faster than a speeding bullet.

The key to most of the reds in this part of Italy, including Chianti, is the Sangiovese grape. It's at its lightest in the inexpensive vini da tavola you'll find in every Tuscan supermarket, and at its richest and most expensive in two DOCGs, Brunello di Montalcino and Vino Nobile di Montepulciano. Both these wines need some serious aging to allow their acidity and tannin to soften, but there are sort of junior versions, Rosso di Montalcino and Rosso di Montepulciano, which are softer and can be drunk younger. Morellino di Scansano has good, light cherry fruit; Carmignano is elegant and seriously good.

Apple-fresh, plum-rich Montepulciano (not to be confused with the Tuscan town of the same name) is the other major red grape of central Italy. Montepulciano d'Abruzzo is good, gutsy stuff at it's best. Tasty Rosso Conero and Rosso Piceno from Marche blend it with Sangiovese.

Whites are light, dry and neutral in these parts: Vernaccia di San Gimignano, Verdicchio, Frascati, Orvieto are the best known. They can all be very attractive, but apart from the top wines, you can treat them interchangeably. Lambrusco is light, fizzy white or red. The best is dry with a lipsmacking sharp bite, but most exported Lambrusco is sweetened, and pretty insipid as a result.

Do regions matter?

With the exception of the Super-Tuscans and 'designer' wines (see below), Tuscany has one basic style of red. Think of the regions as a hierarchy of quality and price. At the top are Vino Nobile di Montepulciano and Brunello di Montalcino. Just below, you've got Chianti Classico and Carmignano, then the rest of Chianti. Below them come simpler DOCs like Morellino de Scansano, then the everyday vini da tavola. Montepulciano-based reds taste different: richer, but coarser with it. The whites all taste much the same at the everyday level, but good Verdicchios and Orvietos are class acts.

Do vintages matter?

Yes, for the better reds. See the Quick Guide, right.

When do I drink them?

Whites are best as everyday wines. Drink the reds with robust food – it's what they were made for. Really good reds deserve a few years' bottle age.

Can I afford them?

Yes and no. Top quality reds hit the investment market. Less expensive wines are good value, and so individual that you can't afford not to try them.

Wine terms | **Super-Tuscans and modern 'designer' wines**

There was once an Italian wine law which, among other absurdities, forced Tuscan producers to add white grapes to their Chianti. Top producers couldn't stand it and they started a rebellion. They made no effort to comply with the rules and instead experimented with grape varieties that were forbidden for DOC wines, like Cabernet Sauvignon, and aging wine in new oak barrels, which was also forbidden. They classified the wines as simple vini da tavola, gave them fancy names, like Sassicaia or Tignanello, and charged a fortune for them. The wines became known as **Super-Tuscans** or **Super Vini da Tavola**. Now, the law has changed and some of them have become DOC or, more commonly, IGT. But those top producers have never stopped experimenting and are famed for both traditional wines like Chianti and highly fashionable ones made from international grapes, including Cabernet, Syrah, Merlot, Pinot Noir, Chardonnay and Viognier.

Quick guide | Central Italy

Location These are the wine regions forming the calf of Italy's boot shape. Tuscany is the most significant.

Grapes Principally Sangiovese for the reds. Montepulciano is grown in Marche and Abruzzo. Trebbiano, Verdicchio and Vernaccia are the main whites. Cabernet Sauvignon and Chardonnay are well established and producers are experimenting with many international varieties.

Local jargon *Riserva* – wine with extra aging before release. *Classico* – the central, best part of a region. *Rufina* – the best Chianti subzone after Chianti Classico. Others are Colli Aretini, Colli Fiorentini, Colli Senesi, Colline Pisane, Montalbano.

Vintages to look for 1998, 1997, 1996, 1995, 1993, 1990, 1988, 1985.

Vintages to avoid 1992 is generally best avoided.

EMILIA-ROMAGNA   PO   ADRIATIC SEA
UMBRIA
TUSCANY   ①   ②MARCHE
③   ABRUZZO
Rome   LAZIO   MOLISE

① Chianti
② Verdicchio
③ Orvieto

Ten to try
Red
- **Cornacchia** Montepulciano d'Abruzzo ②
- **Castello di Brolio** Chianti Classico ②
- **Avignonesi** Vino Nobile di Montepulciano ③
- **Col d'Orcia** Rosso di Montalcino ③
- **Umani Ronchi** Rosso Conero, Cúmaro ③
- **Castellare** Chianti Classico Riserva ③
- **Argiano** Brunello di Montalcino ④
- **Isole e Olena** Cepparello ⑤
White
- **La Carraia** Orvieto ②
- **Antinori** Cervaro della Sala ④

Wine terms | Vin santo

Traditionally a Tuscan speciality but made all over Italy, **vin santo** (holy wine) is produced from dried Trebbiano, Malvasia and other grapes. It can be dry or sweet, depending on whether it is intended as an apéritif or a dessert wine. The best truly are divine – sweet wines with a taste of nuts, dried apricots and crystallized orange peel.

MAIN PICTURE *Rolling hills, poplars, villas and vineyards all contribute to the magical attraction of Tuscany.*

Quick guide | Southern Italy

Location Puglia, Campania, Basilicata and Calabria, which make up the toe and heel of Italy's boot, plus the islands of Sicily, Sardinia, Pantelleria and Lipari.

Grapes Almondy Aglianico, dark, glowering Negroamaro and rich Nero d'Avola are the most exciting reds, followed by burly, peppery Primitivo. Cannonau is a Sardinian relative of Grenache. Local whites include Greco, Fiano, Torbato, Nuragus, Vermentino, Vernaccia, Malvasia and Catarratto. Muscat produces delicious sweet wines.

① Salice Salentino
② Copertino
③ Marsala

Fortified regions Marsala, Moscato di Pantelleria.

Ten to try
Red
• **Candido** Salice Salentino ②
• **Cantina Copertino** Copertino ②
• **Santadi** Monica di Sardegna ②
• **Fratelli d'Angelo** Aglianico del Vulture ②

• **Planeta** Santa Cecilia ④
• **Caggiano** Taurasi ⑤
• **Duca di Salaparuta** Duca Enrico ⑤
White
• **Cantele** Chardonnay Barrique ②
• **Sella e Mosca** Vermentino di Sardegna, La Cala ②
• **De Bartoli** Vecchio Samperi ③

De Bartoli's Vecchio Samperi is a bone-dry, unfortified style of Marsala. Candido's Salice Salentino is an excellent-value red.

Southern Italy

I think I love this part of Italy most of all. The wines are just so good. They're not expensive, but they're stuffed with flavour, unrestrained and slightly wild. They couldn't taste more Italian if they tried.

In other words, it's an up-and-coming region, and it's coming up so fast I can hardly keep pace with it. The reds are the thing: they're sturdy, spicy and chocolaty, with a touch of prunes and raisins and roast coffee beans. Salice Salentino is a wine to look for; so is Copertino. Puglia has led the way, but Sicily is now striding ahead and Sardinia is racing to catch up.

Southern Italy has loads of exciting and individual red grape varieties, like Aglianico, Nero d'Avola and Negroamaro, but this is above all the home of Primitivo, the grape that is generally agreed to be the European ancestor of California's Zinfandel. In some places there are terrific whites, too: Puglia generally makes them from international grapes like Chardonnay, but elsewhere in the South you'll find fascinating herb-scented native varieties. I'm also fond of fortified Marsala, for its brown-sugar sweetness and its tingling acidity, but I like the rare unfortified dry wines even more.

Do regions matter?
Not that much: you'll get southern Italian character pretty much whatever you buy.

Do vintages matter?
Ditto.

When do I drink them?
These are relaxed sort of wines, but they still demand attention. It's a waste to knock them back thoughtlessly. Cook some good rustic Italian food for them.

Can I afford them?
Yes, yes, yes. There are loads of brilliant-value budget wines, and the expensive ones are very classy.

Spain

SPAIN HAS CHANGED. Tired, musty wines are a thing of the past: modern Spain is, well, modern. It's fashionable and it's fashion-conscious. Young, juicy reds are Spain's latest calling card, and I'm all for them. I love these easy-going, glugging wines with their flavours of damsons and strawberries. La Mancha, Valdepeñas, Valencia, Tarragona and Jumilla are all turning out tasty examples, as well as the regions I look at in detail in this chapter.

I love the more serious reds, too: spicy, warm-hearted ones where the damsons have a streak of cloves and cream and a backbone of ripe tannin. And I like the whites, now that they're bright and fresh and full of grassy, leafy fruit.

The best of old Spain hasn't disappeared, though. Rioja still has its soft, strawberry- and cream-scented reds and custardy oak-aged whites. And good sherry has some of the most startling flavours you'll ever find in a wine bottle.

Rioja

Rioja is the most traditional of Spanish wine regions. That doesn't mean that nothing has changed, but Rioja is still the wine to go for if you like the flavours of old Spain: the vanilla and strawberries, the mature, leathery taste of the reds. There are plenty of young reds being made in Rioja, too, but they haven't ousted the traditional styles.

If you want old-style white Rioja with lots of barrel age and a yellow tinge to the colour, that's more difficult to find. Most producers make white Rioja in a more modern green, tangy style, with lemony-crisp

BAY OF BISCAY

RÍAS BAIXAS

NAVARRA

RIOJA

SOMONTANO

TORO

RIBERA DEL DUERO

Duero

Barcelona

PEÑEDES

RUEDA

PRIORAT

TARRAGONA

• Madrid

LA MANCHA

VALENCIA

VALDEPEÑAS

JUMILLA

MONTILLA MORILES

• Seville

JEREZ Y MANZANILLA

N

0 km   200
0 miles   100   200

MEDITERRANEAN SEA

SPANISH CLASSIFICATIONS

The Spanish system, like all EU systems, has layers of quality. And like Italy, Spain has an extra, top tier.

Denominación de Origen Calificada (DOC) This is a super-category reserved for wines with a long tradition of high quality. So far only Rioja has been awarded the DOC accolade.

Denominación de Origen (DO) The standard designation for quality wine applies to over 50 regions, with fairly strict regulations regarding things like grape varieties and yields.

Vino de la tierra These regions are akin to the French vin de pays regions for wines that should have regional character. Many have ambitions to be promoted to DO status. Wine from less closely defined regions with less rigorous standards is known as *vino comarcal*.

Vino de mesa As in other European countries the most basic wines are known as table wine.

Quick guide | Rioja and the North-East

Location Rioja and Navarra are neighbouring regions in the North. Somontano, Penedès and Priorat are further east.

Grapes Red Rioja is traditionally a blend of Tempranillo and Garnacha (the Spanish for Grenache), sometimes with some Graciano and Mazuelo. You'll find Tempranillo and Garnacha everywhere else too, and Cariñena (Spanish for Carignan), but also international varieties. Styles range from juicy, fruity to spicy and warm-hearted. The traditional white grapes of Rioja are Viura and Malvasía, and you'll find Parellada, Xarel-lo and Macabeo (aka Viura) in Cataluña in the east, plus international varieties.

Local jargon *Joven* – young. *Sin crianza* ('without aging') means much the same thing; the wine is sold in the first or second year after the vintage. *Crianza* – with a year or a bit more in barrel and bottle. *Reserva* – at least three years' aging in barrel and bottle. *Gran Reserva* – at least four years' aging. White Reservas and Gran Reservas have less aging than this.

Vintages to look for (Rioja) 1996, 1995, 1994.

Twenty to try
Red
- **Principe de Viana** Navarra, Agramont 1
- **Guelbenzu** Navarra Crianza 2
- **Baso** Navarra 1

BAY OF BISCAY

MEDITERRANEAN SEA

① Rioja
② Navarra   ④ Penedès
③ Somontano ⑤ Priorat

- **Artadi** Rioja, Orobio 2
- **Enate** Somontano Crianza 2
- **Palacio Glorioso** Rioja Crianza 2
- **Raïmat** Costers del Segre, Abadía 2 or Costers del Segre, Mas Castell
- **Campillo** Rioja Reserva 3
- **Scala Dei** Priorat Negre 3
- **Remelluri** Rioja Reserva 3
- **Chivite** Navarra, Colección 125 Reserva 3
- **CVNE** Rioja, Imperial Gran Reserva 4
- **Costers del Siurana** Priorat, Clos de l'Obac 5
White
- **Torres** Penedès, Viña Sol 1
- **Nekeas** Navarra, Chardonnay 2
- **Viñas del Vero** Somontano, Barrel-Fermented Chardonnay 2
- **Marqués de Murrieta** Rioja Reserva 2
Rosé
- **Ochoa** Garnacha Rosé 2
Sparkling white
- **Codorníu** Cava, Cuvée Raventos 2

fruit. The more traditional wines are intense and nutty. The best go vegetal and creamy, not unlike mature white Burgundy, but with a pungent sour-cream finish.

Do regions matter?

Not really. Rioja Alta and Rioja Alavesa are the best sub-regions, but most Riojas are a blend of grapes from all over the region.

Do vintages matter?

They do for the top wines. See the Quick Guide, opposite. But don't bother about vintages for the young wines.

When do I drink them?

Absolutely any time. They're tasty enough for any occasion, though the finer red Riojas are more serious wines that deserve good food, and really top traditional white Rioja might come as a shock to somebody who didn't know what to expect. The light reds are good for summer.

Can I afford them?

Usually. Rioja, however, is becoming more expensive than its quality always deserves and the best wines (labelled Gran Reserva) will be pretty expensive. Simple young Riojas no longer offer the same value as reds from elsewhere in Spain.

Modern north-east Spain

There could hardly be a better overview than this of what's been happening to Spanish wine in recent years. Navarra, once a sort of understudy to Rioja, is a hotbed of experimentation: so much so that there's no easy-to-define single style. There are young juicy, fruity reds and oak-aged, mature wines; there are varietal wines and there are blends; there are traditional Spanish grapes like

The wine region of Rioja lies in the Ebro Valley in north-east Spain, bounded by the dramatic Sierra de Cantabria mountains.

Garnacha and Tempranillo, and there are international ones like Cabernet and Chardonnay. There are plenty of crisp whites and strawberryish *rosados* (the Spanish term for rosé), too.

Penedès was the first region in Spain to plant international grape varieties like Chardonnay and Cabernet Sauvignon, and the first to make distinctively international-style wines. Whites were, and are, in both the ripe and toasty and green and tangy styles; reds were and are intense and blackcurranty or spicy and brawny. Some are varietals; others are blends of international and Spanish grapes. Nearby Costers del Segre also has a good line in ripe, spicy reds and toasty whites.

Penedès hasn't always kept up with the trends since its initial advances, but Somontano has taken a headlong rush for modernity. It's growing international grapes for all its worth, and making varietals from Cabernet Sauvignon, Merlot, Pinot Noir, Gewürztraminer and Chardonnay. And it's making them with remarkable finesse and delicacy.

In Priorat change has gone even further, albeit in a different direction. This region is one of the new stars of Spanish wine. The best wines are developing a cult following, and prices have soared sky-high. It's because a group of big-time investors spotted the potential of the area and set about making the very best wines they could. They keep yields right down and pick practically grape by grape for their best wines. These are spicy, warm-hearted reds with a vengeance. There are, however, some affordable reds that are still wonderfully gutsy and in the same mould, and even some juicy young wines.

I mustn't forget Cava. Cava is simply the Spanish term for traditional-method sparkling wine, and while it can come from almost anywhere in the North-East, in practice most comes from Penedès. Don't expect it to taste like Champagne. These days there might be some Chardonnay in the blend to give a bit more refinement, but the basic grapes are Parellada, Macabeo and Xarel-lo, none of which is ever going to be in the running for a Best White Grape of the Year award. At best Cava is pleasant, clean and fresh – some of the world's best-value fizz. Poor Cavas are earthy and rooty, and they'll ruin a good party.

Do regions matter?
Not within any of the regions I've outlined above.

Do vintages matter?
No.

When do I drink them?
Only drink the cult wines of Priorat if you're being treated to dinner by a millionaire. Otherwise these are wines for pretty well any occasion, and Penedès and Costers del Segre have some tasty reds and whites that will do for the smartest of parties.

Can I afford them?
Er, mostly. Top Penedès wines are expensive and not always worth it; varietals from Somontano are very good value – but that doesn't mean dirt cheap. The same goes for Navarra. The young wines everywhere are good value. As for the top Priorats, well, I expect you've got the message by now.

North-west Spain

Okay, here's a diverse bunch to get your teeth into. These wines range from rich, concentrated reds to light, aromatic whites. They show the two extremes of what Spain is doing today, but they have one thing in common: they are all highly fashionable in Spain itself, and that always gets prices moving – upwards.

First stop, Ribera del Duero. These wines are usually entirely Tempranillo, aged partly in new oak, with a vanilla-and-spice dimension to the bright, blackcurrant

Rías Baixas is in the most verdant part of North-West Spain, where vineyards run down to the shores of huge estuaries, known as rías.

fruit. Quality is high and getting higher, though prices are generally rather higher than the quality justifies. The wines age well; indeed they demand some aging for the tannins to soften.

Next, Toro. This can be thought of as a sort of junior Ribera del Duero in flavour: plummier, more robust, perhaps without quite the focused flavour, but still a hell of a mouthful of palate-blasting fruit. Toro is quite good value, though prices have risen.

Rueda is arguably Spain's leading white wine region. Flavours are green and tangy; quality reliable. You might think, from a quick taste, that they're all made from

Sauvignon Blanc, and you wouldn't be far wrong: there is some Sauvignon here, though the major grape is Verdejo. Some is aged in oak for a more butter-and-toast flavour.

Rías Baixas is Spain's other candidate in the good white wine stakes. These aromatic, apricotty wines generally come from the Albariño grape. Not all have the sort of elegance and lightness that I expect – and they're expensive. Similar wines from Valdeorras, Ribeiro and Ribeira Sacra can be cheaper and more fragrant. So buy them.

Do regions matter?
Only as above.

Do vintages matter?
They do for Ribera del Duero. See the Quick Guide, below.

When do I drink them?
Save Ribera del Duero for people you want to impress; give Toro and Rueda to people you like. They all go well with food. Rías Baixas is best on its own or as an apéritif.

Can I afford them?
You can afford Toro and Rueda best. Ribera del Duero goes all the way up to astronomical. Look for Valdeorras, Ribeiro or Ribeira Sacra if you can't stretch to Rías Baixas.

Quick guide | North-west Spain

Location *Most of these regions are located along the River Duero.*
Grapes Reds – Tempranillo; whites – Sauvignon Blanc, Verdejo and Albariño.

Local jargon *Reserva* – red with extra aging before release. Should be higher quality. *Gran Reserva* – red with lots of extra aging before release. Should be much higher quality.

Vintages to look for (Ribera del Duero) 1996, 1995, 1994, 1991, 1990.

Vintages to avoid (Ribera del Duero) 1993.

Ten to try
Red
• **Frutos Villar** Toro, Miralmonte Crianza 2
• **Fariña** Toro, Gran Collegiata Reserva 2
• **Pesquera** Ribera del Duero, Condado de Haza 2

BAY OF BISCAY

Valladolid

① Rías Baixas   ③ Toro
② Ribera del Duero   ④ Rueda

• **Pago de Carraovejas** Ribera del Duero 2
• **Viña Pedrosa** Ribera del Duero Reserva 4
• **Vega Sicilia** Ribera del Duero, Alión Reserva 4
White
• **Marqués de Riscal** Rueda 2
• **Bodegas Godeval** Valdeorras, Viña Godeval 2
• **Belondrade y Lurton** Rueda 3
• **Pazo de Senorans** Rías Baixas, Albariño 3

Quick guide | Sherry

Location In the south of Spain. The region's official name is Jerez y Manzanilla. See the map on page 101.

Grapes Most sherry is made from Palomino, which makes incredibly boring unfortified wine. But turned into sherry it's fabulous. The other grape (and the main one in Montilla) is Pedro Ximénez (or PX), which makes wonderfully grapy sweet sherry.

Local jargon *Dulce* – sweet. *Muy dulce* – very sweet. *Muy viejo* – very old. *Seco* – dry. *Almacenista* – small-scale producer with just a few barrels of high-quality sherry. The company of Emilio Lustau makes a speciality of bottling these.

Ten to try
Fino and manzanilla
- **Barbadillo** Manzanilla de Sanlúcar ①
- **Domecq** La Ina ②
- **Hidalgo** La Gitana ②
- **Valdespino** Inocente ②
Amontillado
- **Hidalgo** Napoleon ②
- **Valdespino** Coliseo ③
- **González Byass** Del Duque ④
Oloroso
- **Williams & Humbert** Dos Cortados ②
- **González Byass** Matusalem (sweet) ⑤
- **Osborne** Solera India ⑤

Sherry takes years to develop its unique flavours and the atmosphere in the bodega must be carefully regulated.

Sherry

I've got news for you: sherry doesn't have to taste a bit like that sweetish brown concoction we've all endured at some time. That was sherry dumbed down for export. Sherry as the Spanish drink it is altogether different. For one thing, it's bone dry. For another, it's intensely aromatic, smelling of bread yeast and apple cores, nuts and prunes, coffee and toast. It's one of the great fortified wines of the world.

Dry sherry can be light and pale (*fino* or *manzanilla*), darker and more concentrated (*amontillado*) or darker and more concentrated still (*oloroso*).

Good sweet sherries do exist. The Pedro Ximénez grape makes intensely grapy, scented wine that is almost black in colour. The Spanish drink this with dessert, or pour it over ice cream. Other good sweet sherries will have the Spanish word *dulce* on the label, or *muy dulce*, meaning very sweet. Spanish words like this – *muy viejo* for very old, or *seco* for dry – are a good sign: they indicate that the same wine is sold on the Spanish market, to people who are serious about the quality of their sherry.

Montilla makes wines similar in style and flavour to sherry, though it seldom has the bite of good sherry.

Do regions matter?
Get to grips with styles before you worry about regions.

Do vintages matter?
All sherry is non-vintage. It is produced by the solera system, which basically means that you have a series of barrels of wine at different stages of maturity. You bottle wine from the most mature barrel, but you take only a proportion of the barrel. You top up the barrel from the next most mature barrel, and so on until you reach the youngest, which you top up with new wine. Every bottle of sherry is therefore a blend of wine of almost all ages.

When do I drink it?
Fino is a perfect apéritif, and ideal with tapas. Dry *amontillado* or dry *oloroso* make good winter apéritifs, when it seems a bit dark and cold for *fino*; and really good sweet sherries are excellent after dinner. Drink *fino* fast: ideally, buy half bottles and polish them off in one go.

Can I afford them?
Good sherry is terrifically cheap for the quality.

Portugal

PORTUGAL IS JUST discovering itself, in wine terms. Yes, port and Madeira are among the great sweet fortified wines of the world, but the table wines, red and white, are only now finding their feet. And they have flavours, especially in the reds, that you'll find nowhere else: of chocolate, damsons and vanilla; soft and juicy, yet slightly sour.

Good reds come from the Douro Valley, where they would otherwise be fortified and turned into port; from Dão and Bairrada, where the flavour is herbier; and from the South, especially Alentejo and Ribatejo and their sub-regions, where the wines are often fairly simple but where there are increasing numbers of serious estates.

The whites are generally less exciting, but they can be fresh and attractive. And Portugal can and does produce some very serious whites that age to gain rich, dry flavours of honey and lanolin. They come from individual quality-conscious producers rather than any particular region.

Portugal's most distinctive white table wine is Vinho Verde. The stuff that gets exported in dumpy bottles is generally sweetened: the Vinho Verde I want is bone dry and pungent with apricots and laurel, and has piercing acidity. It's not that easy to find, but it does exist.

And if you like slightly sweet rosé, you could do worse than choose Portuguese. It's better than most.

Do regions matter?

Northern regions like Douro, Dão and Bairrada are noticeably different from the southern regions.

Do vintages matter?

Only rarely, and only in the North.

When do I drink them?

When do you not? These wines are so deliciously different you'll want to drink them all the time. Proper dry Vinho Verde is best with seafood.

Can I afford them?

Yes, yes, yes. The wines of the South are still extremely cheap for the quality. Those of the Douro can be pricier but are generally worth it.

Port and Madeira

Both these famous wines are fortified, but they are totally different. Port is sweet and nutty, and vintage port is full of black fruits, pepper and spice; Madeira is tangy and pungent with a dry finish, even when it's sweet.

Port styles are basically divided between vintage and non-vintage ports. Vintage port comes from a single year, and only in the best years do the producers 'declare' a vintage. The wines should be matured in bottle for ten or 15 years before being opened. Single-quinta vintage ports are a variation on this theme: they come from the best estate owned by the producer, but are made in the second-best years. They are ready to drink at about ten years old.

---

essentials

PORTUGUESE CLASSIFICATIONS

The top tier of quality, the equivalent of France's Appellation Contrôlée, is **Denominação de Origem Controlada**, or DOC. **IPR** (sometimes labelled VQPRD) is below that. Then comes **vinho regional**, the equivalent of French vin de pays, and table wine is **vinho de mesa**.

LBV, or Late-Bottled Vintage, is rather different. Yes, it's wine from a single year, but it's usually over-processed. 'Traditional' unfiltered LBV, however, is a lovely, perfumed drink that can be enjoyed as soon as you buy it.

Crusted is a non-vintage blend that is usually an excellent budget substitute for vintage port; vintage character is mostly undistinguished stuff. Tawny is the most wonderful of the non-vintage styles. Ten-Year-Old tawny combines maturity with freshness; 20-Year-Old is nuttier and more mature; and 40-Year-Old is very nutty indeed.

Then there are the ports that simply have a proprietary name, like His Excellency's Frightfully Old Port. Some of these are good, but many are just glorified cheap rubies and tawnies. Read the back label carefully for clues. If it says Ruby, it's the simplest and youngest of ports, and no power on earth will ever turn it into anything better.

Madeira is classified quite differently. Here levels of sweetness are the key. Sercial is the lightest and driest; Verdelho is slightly weightier and off-dry. Bual is fairly sweet and rich, and Malmsey is very sweet. All get their pungent, smoky tang from they way they are heat-treated, so that the wine gently oxidises. It's not a flavour you'd welcome in other wines, but in Madeira it's essential.

Do regions matter?

No.

Do vintages matter?

Only for vintage port. Most Madeira is non-vintage.

When do I drink them?

At the end of the day, unless you want to fall asleep. The Portuguese drink tawny as an apéritif; dry Madeira is also a good apéritif. Vintage port deserves serious treatment, not to mention a lie-in the next morning.

Can I afford them?

Good ports and Madeiras aren't cheap, and poor ones aren't worth the hangover.

Quick guide | Portugal

Location Vinho Verde, port, Dão and Bairrada are from the North, but the upcoming regions are further south in Ribatejo, Alentejo and Estremadura. Madeira is an island west of Morocco.

Grapes The secret of Portugal's flavours is its abundance of indigenous grapes found nowhere else. Few of these grapes' names appear on labels, but Touriga Nacional, Baga and Tinta Roriz (Tempranillo) are good red grapes whose names you might see. The main Madeira grapes are Sercial, Verdelho, Bual and Malmsey: each of the different styles is made from the grape of that name.

Local jargon *Quinta* – estate. *5/10/20/40-Year-Old* – Age statements refer to the average age of the wine in the blend, not to any particular vintage. The age is an indicator of style for tawny port. Only buy Madeira with an age statement, preferably 10-Year-Old, or you won't get the full character.

Vintages to look for (port) 1997, 1994, 1992, 1991, 1985, 1983, 1980.

Ten to try
Red
- **Bright Brothers** Palmela ②
- **Quinta do Crasto** Douro ②
- **Quinta de la Rosa** Douro ②
- **Esporão** Reguengos ②
- **Quinta da Boavista** Alenquer ②
- **Luis Pato** Bairrada, Vinha Pan ④
Port
- **Ramos Pinto** Quinta da Ervamoira 10-Year-Old Tawny ④
- **Taylor** Quinta de Vargellas (single-quinta vintage) ⑤
Madeira
- **Blandy's** 10-Year-Old Verdelho (dry) ④
- **Henriques & Henriques** 10-Year-Old Malmsey (sweet) ④

LEFT AND MAIN PICTURE *Quinta do Crasto in the Douro Valley was one of the first port estates to find success with red wine.*

Germany

Tell me your attitude to German wine, and I'll tell you whether you're a wine snob or not. You see, Germany produces some sensationally good white wines – some of the best in the world. They have elegance, refinement, concentration and they live for decades, maturing to a fascinating honeyed richness. But these vinous wonders have been horribly overshadowed by the fact that Germany also makes some of the worst wines in the world. They're cheap, sugary and the worst of it is, they are made in a style that apes that of the very best wines.

Anybody who has tasted good German wine and fallen in love with it – and the two processes are usually simultaneous – could not possibly mistake the two styles. But several generations of wine drinkers have been brought up to despise German wines because all they've ever tasted is the dross.

The fact that you're reading this chapter indicates that you're prepared to look beyond the received opinions of wine snobs. Read a bit further and I'll tell you how to find those sensationally good wines.

Riesling

The best and simplest guide to quality is the word Riesling on the label. Riesling is the classic white grape of Germany, and it's too costly to grow to be used for the worst wines. Riesling's characteristic flavour in Germany is tangy, though not particularly green; grapy and flowery, sometimes peachy, sometimes appley, sometimes smoky when young, and there's usually some sweetness in the wine to balance the grape's high acidity. That's important, because these are light wines with low levels of alcohol, and the acidity has to be balanced by something.

South of Bonn, vineyards line the banks of the Rhine with green and gold. Few other parts of Germany are warm enough for vines.

Looking at it the other way round, don't be put off by a touch of sweetness in a good Riesling: the acidity makes it delicious rather than cloying.

That's the basic flavour. The picture is complicated by the German system of classification, which grades wines according to the ripeness and natural sweetness of the grapes. The highest grades of wines are invariably very sweet. The lower grades can be dry or off-dry. Most of the wines drunk in Germany itself are made dry, but in good examples a little perfumed fruitiness always peeps through.

GERMAN CLASSIFICATIONS

Tafelwein and **Landwein** are the most basic and not worth bothering with. **Qualitätswein bestimmter Anbaugebiete** (QbA) wines come from one of the country's 13 wine regions. They can be okay, but the infamous Liebfraumilch is a QbA, so beware. The next grade up and the one to look for is **Qualitätswein mit Prädikat** (QmP), and there are six styles. In ascending order of ripeness, sweetness and price they are: Kabinett, Spätlese, Auslese, Beerenauslese, Trockenbeerenauslese and Eiswein. See page 73 for more details.

The kind of area a wine comes from also has a bearing on its likely quality. Single vineyards, or **Einzellagen**, are the ones to go for. On the label you'll see the name of the village with the suffix -er (for example, Bernkasteler from the village of Bernkastel) followed by the name of the vineyard. **Grosslagen** are bigger areas without the same specific character. Grosslagen are very difficult to spot on labels, because they have invented names for themselves that sound just like single vineyards. Niersteiner Gutes Domtal is a Grosslage; Niersteiner Pettenthal is a top vineyard. A **Bereich** is larger again. If the label says, for example, Bereich Bernkastel, the wine is unlikely to be exciting. Bernkastel itself is a top village and produces excellent wine; but the Bereich Bernkastel extends much further and includes some decidedly inferior vineyards.

Quick guide | Germany

Location The wine regions are mostly in the south-west of the country, gathered around the River Rhine and its tributaries.

Grapes Riesling makes the best wines, in a tangy though not green style; Scheurebe is fragrant and grapefruity; Pinot Blanc (or Weissburgunder) is less tangy and more nutty; Pinot Gris (Grauburgunder or Ruländer) is nutty and earthy; Silvaner is dry and neutral. Traminer (Gewürztraminer) is floral. Müller-Thurgau is generally undistinguished. The best red is Pinot Noir (Spätburgunder).

Local jargon *Trocken* – dry. *Halbtrocken* – off-dry. *VDP/Charta* – an organisation of top Rheingau producers. *Sekt* – sparkling wine.

Vintages to look for 1998, 1997, 1996, 1995, 1993, 1990, or any Mosel wine from the 1990s.

Vintages to avoid 1992, apart from the Mosel.

Ten to try
All these producers make a range of wines from various individual estates in their region. Prices begin at 2 for a Kabinett, 3 for a Spätlese. The best and rarest wines are 5.
• **Kurt Darting** Pfalz
• **Hermann Dönnhoff** Nahe
• **Gunderloch** Rheinhessen
• **Fritz Haag** Mosel
• **Toni Jost** Mittelrhein
• **von Kesselstatt** Mosel
• **Franz Künstler** Rheingau
• **J Leitz** Rheingau
• **Dr Loosen** Mosel
• **Müller-Catoir** Pfalz

Certain regions, mostly in the south, produce some red wines, and they can be good; but Germany is fundamentally a white-wine country.

Do regions matter?
They do, very much, but above all stick to good grapes. The best wines usually come from the Mosel (lighter, leaner, smokier wines); the Rheingau (weightier, riper); the Rheinhessen (softer, and with only a small proportion of its vineyards dedicated to good quality); and the Pfalz (big ripe wines, often from Pinot Blanc, Pinot Noir and others as well as Riesling). Baden wines, white or red, can be good – the Pinot family is more important here than Riesling – and Franken grows quite impressive dry Silvaner and fair Müller-Thurgau.

Do vintages matter?
Yes and no. There is certainly great vintage variation, but the system of classification of wines by grape ripeness means that the better grades are only produced when the grapes are ripe enough – so in poor vintages only simple wines will be made. See the Quick Guide, left.

When do I drink them?
The lighter wines – QbAs, Kabinetts, Spätleses – make good apéritifs, but also go well with foods like trout or salmon or crab; with pâté; or with gently spicy Chinese or South-East Asian food. Keep the very sweet wines for puddings or for drinking on their own after dinner. Everybody loves them. But remember that Riesling needs bottle age. Even a light Kabinett will improve for four years or so after the vintage, and the higher grades need longer.

Can I afford them?
Luckily, yes. Prices for top producers are high because demand is high in Germany, but it's still possible to buy a very good quality Kabinett or Spätlese for a much lower price than you would pay for a comparable wine from many other countries.

Other European countries

THIS IS WHERE we get into unfamiliar grape varieties, and flavours which, without being strident, manage to be quite unlike any others. Vineyards crop up across the continent from the eastern border of Germany right up to the shores of the Black Sea and well beyond. And to the north, a few spots in England and Wales have what it takes to grow decent grapes.

England and Wales

Most wines are white and vary from dry to off-dry; the most successful seem to me to fall into two categories. On the one hand there are the light, dry, rather neutral wines with the capacity to age; Seyval Blanc is a useful grape for this style. On the other, the scented, green and tangy ones. Some are heavily aromatic, with perfumes of pot pourri or elderflower. When they're in balance these wines can be a delight, but they quickly pall if made too sugary. The best sparkling wines, like Nyetimber, are outstanding, but many tend to be a bit green-tasting and unripe. Overall quality is unreliable, though improving.

Austria

Austria may classify its wines in much the same way as Germany (with one or two differences), but the basic style of Austrian wine is not the same. Most wines in Germany are light and low in alcohol, and may be dry or medium depending on the producer. Austrian wines are basically dry, but riper and weightier, and noticeably higher in alcohol. Whites can be neutral, green and tangy, or intense and nutty; reds are mostly juicy and peppery, though the more serious of them discard that instant juiciness in favour of greater structure concealed beneath velvet fruit. And when Austria makes wines sweet, they are very sweet: rich, honeyed, complex and highly concentrated.

Different regions have different styles. The best, fruitiest, most velvety reds come from Burgenland, as do the intense sweet wines; the Neusiedlersee is the spot for these. Dry whites here are pretty good, too. Steiermark goes to the other extreme, with wines that are light and acidic to the point of hurting your gums. Niederösterreich produces subtle, firm whites with good fragrance: Wachau is the region for superb Riesling. Niederösterreich also produces the best Grüner Veltliner, Austria's everyday glugging white. Light and appetising, it has a flavour of pepper and bay leaves and is often very good quality.

Switzerland

There are three basic styles of wine made in Switzerland: French, German and Italian. The best wines are nearly all French-style, made in the French-speaking regions. The dominant white grape is the neutral Chasselas; reds are

RIGHT *Nyetimber is made in the same way as Champagne.* CENTRE RIGHT *The Ausbruch classification for sweet wine is unique to Austria.*

CENTRE LEFT *Swiss Pinot Noir is lighter than Burgundy.* LEFT *Naoussa is a spicy warm-hearted Greek wine made with Xynomavro grapes.*

mostly light, jammy Gamay or Pinot Noir, or often a blend of the two, such as Dôle. They don't taste as good as Burgundy or Beaujolais, but they cost as much.

So what should one look for? Well, the Chasselas whites can be surprisingly tasty. Otherwise, try to find some of Switzerland's speciality grapes, such as Petite Arvine, Amigne and Humagne Blanc. These produce rich, dry wines – sometimes sweet ones, too – and the first two are headily perfumed. The Valais region also manages some good Chardonnay and Syrah.

Whites from German-speaking Switzerland are mostly made from Müller-Thurgau, known here as Riesling-Sylvaner. It's a grape that is no more capable of producing top quality wines than it is of flying to the moon. There are also a few light, smoky reds. Italian-speaking Switzerland makes soft, occasionally impressive Merlot.

Greece

Greece has grape varieties grown nowhere else. And good grape varieties, too: you'll see names like Robola, Roditis and Moscophilero on the labels of the whites; Xynomavro, Limnio or Aghiorghitiko on the reds. The whites are green and tangy, with a crisp lemony flavour and good acidity and weight, though Moscophilero is aromatic and Muscat is usually sweet. The reds are spicy and warmhearted, full-bodied and assertive.

Eastern Europe

The countries of Eastern Europe produce both modern, New World-influenced wines and traditional styles from indigenous grapes – and while at the moment the cheap and reliable New World flavours are probably the best value, we ought to see more and more exciting native styles as year by year they get their vineyards and their winemaking sorted out.

Bulgaria has good-value copies of classic French styles, using Cabernet Sauvignon, Merlot and some passable Chardonnay; Mavrud, Gamza and Melnik are also good varieties for slightly jammy, juicy reds. Quality can be a bit up and down but the wines are inexpensive, so experimentation won't break the bank.

Hungary has the rose-scented white Irsai Olivér and red Kadarka and Kékfrankos, the latter full of redcurrant fruit when it's well-made. There are also an increasing number of excellent examples of international grapes like Sauvignon Blanc, Chardonnay and Pinot Gris. At the moment these are just attractive, everyday gluggers, but Hungary's long-term potential is enormous. Tokaji, Hungary's fabulous sweet wine, perfumed with smoke, beeswax, orange peel and honey, has been famous for centuries and is leading the way.

In Romania there's uneven quality and low prices; reds can be soft and jammy, whites balanced and nutty at their best. Very good sweet wines come from the Tămîioasă grape; other good grapes include the aromatic Fetească. The Czech Republic and Slovakia aren't big exporters, but both have light, gently spicy whites. Slovenia has good, weighty whites from Laski Rizling and Pinot Blanc, tangy Sauvignon Blanc and some juicy reds.

Do regions matter?

Most regions only have one major winery. If the winery's good, the region's good.

Do vintages matter?

Freshness can be a problem, so in general stick to the most recent vintage you can find.

When do I drink them?

Mostly they're everyday wines. Tokaji is for special occasions and after dinner.

Can I afford them?

Good Tokaji is expensive and prices are relatively high in Slovenia, but the rest of Eastern Europe has loads of good wine at low prices.

MAIN PICTURE *Tokaji being clarified by a process called racking: the wine is transferred to a fresh barrel, leaving any solid deposits behind in the old one.*

Quick guide | Eastern Europe

Location Bulgaria, Hungary and Romania are the main exporters. Moldova, the Czech and Slovak Republics and Slovenia also have good wine.

Grapes Bulgaria has lots of Cabernet Sauvignon, Merlot, Gamza, Mavrud and Melnik for blackcurranty reds of fair intensity or for juicy, fruity styles. Whites are patchier in quality; there's a fair bit of Chardonnay. Hungary has Furmint and Hárslevelü for Tokaji; Irsai Olivér, Kékfrankos, Kékoporto and others for aromatic whites and soft reds; it has international grapes, too. Romania has Pinot Noir, Chardonnay and others, plus the indigenous Fetească and Tămîioasă; Slovenia has Laski Rizling, Pinot Blanc, Sauvignon Blanc and others.

Ten to try

Bulgarian red
- **Iambol** or **Sliven** Merlot ①
- **Lovico Suhindol** or **Russe** Cabernet Sauvignon ①

Bulgarian white
- **Domaine Boyar** Barrel-Fermented Preslav Chardonnay ①

Hungarian white
- **Chapel Hill** Irsai Olivér ① or Chardonnay ①
- **Hilltop** Neszmély Region Sauvignon Blanc ①
- **Royal Tokaji Wine Company** Tokaji Aszú, 5 Puttonyos (sweet) ⑤

Romanian white
- **Pietroasele** Tămîioasă (sweet) ①

Wine terms | Tokaji

Hungary's delicious sweet wine is uniquely tangy and smoky. It is made using grapes with a high level of natural sugar (usually the result of noble rot, the fungus that concentrates the sugar in grapes) which are known as **Aszú**. These wines are labelled **Tokaji Aszú** and the sweetness is measured in **puttonyos**. A three-puttonyos Tokaji is sweet, six is concentrated and rich. **Aszú Eszencia** is sweeter still and very intense. **Szamorodni** contains only a small proportion of Aszú grapes and ranges from dry to medium-sweet.

United States

THE USA IS WHERE the modern wine revolution – the movement that has delivered clean, fresh, fruity-flavoured wine from all around the globe at affordable prices – began. It began, to be precise, in California, where the warm, dry climate is worlds away from that of the classic European regions. But late-20th-century technology provided the key, and the local viticultural centre, the University of California at Davis, provided the know-how and a stream of highly-trained winemakers.

The result has been wines which in the 1970s challenged the domination of Europe, in the 1980s led the charge for change and which now confidently set their own agenda. Wine is produced in many other states, foremost among them Washington, Oregon and New York. But in terms of both quality and quantity, California is way out in the lead.

California

These are generally big, ripe wines, ultra-modern in style. What California does brilliantly is produce an enormous range of wines from a relatively narrow selection of grape varieties. Cabernet Sauvignon, Merlot and California's speciality grape, Zinfandel, rule for reds, often in the intense, blackcurranty or spicy, warm-hearted styles; ripe, toasty Chardonnay accounts for most of the whites; Riesling and Sauvignon Blanc are also widely grown, though they tend to be less tangy than their counterparts elsewhere. The latter in particular may be aged in new oak for a softer, spicier taste, and it works pretty well. These wines are often labelled Fumé Blanc.

Wines can be simple and mass-produced, or rich, complex and expensive, and made in artisan quantities. What

OPPOSITE Modern technology, such as these refrigerated fermentation vats at the Mondavi winery in Oakville, was the key that unlocked California's potential.

US CLASSIFICATIONS

The first **American Viticultural Areas** (AVAs) were introduced in 1983 to impose some degree of classification on the rapidly developing US wine industry. They indicate only the area of origin of a wine and impose no regulations on its quality. They also require honest labelling of grape varieties. In general, the name of the producer is a surer guide to both style and quality when you are buying wine.

Quick guide | California

Location The West Coast of the USA.

Grapes Intense, blackcurranty reds come from Cabernet Sauvignon, sometimes blended with Merlot, or from Merlot on its own. There's good Pinot Noir in a few cool spots. Zinfandel comes in many styles: the best are spicy and warm-hearted. The spicy style also belongs to blends of Syrah, Mourvèdre and Grenache. Sangiovese and other Italian grapes tend to be spicy, too. Whites are most often ripe and toasty. Grapes are Chardonnay, Sauvignon Blanc and Riesling, with the last tending to be soft and fruity rather than tangy.

Vintages to look for 1999, 1998, 1997, 1995, 1994, 1992.

Twenty to try
Red
- **Cline Cellars** California Zinfandel ②
- **Ridge** Coastal Range Zinfandel ③
- **Ravenswood** Sonoma Valley Zinfandel ③
- **Saintsbury** Pinot Noir ③
- **Au Bon Climat** Santa Barbara County Pinot Noir ③
- **Qupé** Syrah ③
- **Beringer** Knight's Valley Cabernet Sauvignon ④
- **Bonny Doon** Le Cigare Volant ④
- **Beaulieu Vineyard** Georges de Latour Cabernet Sauvignon ⑤
- **Matanzas Creek** Merlot ⑤

- **Laurel Glen** Cabernet Sauvignon ⑤
- **Spottswoode** Cabernet Sauvignon ⑤
- **Caymus** Cabernet Sauvignon ⑤
White
- **Clos du Bois** Sonoma Chardonnay ②
- **Beringer** Napa Valley Chardonnay ②
- **Newton** Red Label Chardonnay ④
- **Calera** Viognier ④
- **Kistler** Sonoma Valley Chardonnay ⑤
Sparkling
- **Mumm** Cuvée Napa Brut ③
- **Roederer Estate** Anderson Valley Brut ③
Sweet fortified
- **Quady** Elysium Black Muscat ③

Ten for starters
Exciting California wine is expensive. These less costly wines give an idea of the styles, but don't expect the thrills of the main selection.
Red
- **Sutter Home** Zinfandel ①
- **Cline Cellars** Côtes d'Oakley ①
- **Pepperwood Grove** Cabernet Franc ②
- **Redwood Trail** Pinot Noir ②
- **Fetzer** Zinfandel ②
- **Marietta** Old Vine Red Lot 22 ②
White
- **Glen Ellen** Chardonnay ①
- **Fetzer** Viognier ②
- **St-Supéry** Sauvignon Blanc ②
- **Fetzer** Mendocino Barrel Select Chardonnay ②

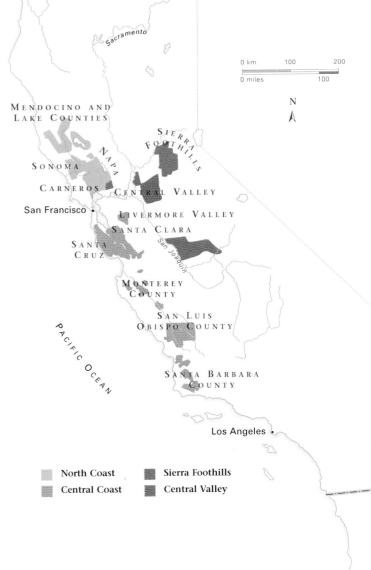

North Coast • Central Coast • Sierra Foothills • Central Valley

 Wine terms | **Meritage**

California producers introduced this marketing term to describe wines made from the same grape varieties as the classic wines of Bordeaux in France. It can apply to both red wines blended from **Cabernet Sauvignon, Merlot** and **Cabernet Franc** and to white **Sauvignon Blanc/Semillon** blends. However, it's rare to see the term on the wine label: as most meritage wines are sold instead under a suitably dignified proprietary name. If a California wine is called anything like Tapestry, Anthology, Elevage, Hommage or Affinity, chances are it's a meritage blend.

you choose depends on how much you want to spend. But be aware that by forking out for the most expensive cult reds you may be paying as much for the ego of the wine-maker as for the quality of the wine: California is a place where you can produce a supposedly world-class super-premium wine simply by saying you will, and by charging a world-class, super-premium price. For wines that are genuinely world-class (and affordable) – and California has plenty – start by looking for a reasonably long track record of quality.

The range of flavours is currently expanding, as more and more producers become interested in the grapes of Italy and the Rhône Valley: Sangiovese is fashionable, as are Syrah, Grenache, Mourvèdre and others. These are big spicy, attention-grabbing reds. The aromatic Rhône white variety Viognier is also becoming popular. Sparkling wines have fallen strongly under the influence of Champagne, partly because so many Champagne houses have set up shop here. A few Sauternes-style sweet Sémillons and sweet fortified Muscats have ultra-ripe fruity flavours.

Zinfandel deserves special consideration. This grape has been shown to be the same variety as Primitivo, a rustic red grape grown in southern Italy. But Zinfandel has achieved renown in a way that Primitivo never did. At its best it makes warming, heavyweight, berry-flavoured reds with soft, ripe tannins; but it is the most amenable of grapes and can make any style you fancy, from soft, juicy gluggers to sweetish pink wine that is usually labelled as 'blush', right up to the burliest of deep reds.

Do regions matter?

AVAs (American Viticultural Areas) on the whole don't matter in the way French AC or Italian DOC regions do. AVAs are delimited appellations, but forget any ideas of a system based on the European model. There are no rules here about what grapes you can grow where, or what styles you should make. This is winemaker heaven: you can make what you want, where you want – just as long as nature will let you and you reckon you can sell it.

Nevertheless, some places are particularly well suited to individual grapes or styles. Napa Valley is California's most famous area. It's where many of the most renowned wineries are based and its red wines, in particular its Cabernet Sauvignons and Merlots, are regarded as California classics. Stags Leap and Rutherford are outstanding sub-regions for Cabernet Sauvignon.

Sonoma County is right next to Napa and is home to excellent whites and reds. The reds are generally a little softer and rounder than those from Napa. Two sub-regions – Dry Creek Valley and Russian River Valley – produce exciting Chardonnay and inspired Zinfandel and Pinot Noir. To the south of Napa and Sonoma, straddling both regions, is Carneros, a cool, foggy region famous for Chardonnay, Pinot Noir and sparkling wine.

South of San Francisco there are vineyard regions sprinkled right down the coast to Los Angeles. Most important of these are Monterey, San Luis Obispo and, in particular, Santa Barbara, including Santa Maria Valley, where some of California's finest Pinot Noir and Chardonnay are grown.

Further inland, the Sierra Foothills produce tub-thumping Zinfandel while the Central Valley (also known as San Joaquin) is a vast agro-industrial area which produces the bulk of California's everyday wine. If the label says North Coast, it means the general region north of San Francisco right up to Mendocino. Central Coast refers to the vineyards south of San Francisco.

Do vintages matter?

Only really for the finest wines and the coolest areas. Vintage variation is never as drastic as in, say, Bordeaux. See the Quick Guide, opposite.

When do I drink them?

Nearly all California wines can be drunk immediately: only the very best will age. Since the very best are startlingly expensive, treat them with the respect due to a hefty outlay of cash and save them for a special occasion.

Quick guide | Washington & Oregon

Location These two states are in the north-west of the USA. Together with neighbouring Idaho they are often referred to as the Pacific Northwest.

Grapes Pinot Noir for reds and Pinot Gris, Pinot Blanc and Chardonnay for whites in Oregon; Cabernet Sauvignon and Merlot are the main Washington reds; white grapes are Chardonnay, Semillon, Riesling and Sauvignon Blanc.

① Willamette Valley
② Yakima Valley
③ Walla Walla

Vintages to look for (Oregon Pinot Noir) 1999, 1996, 1994. Washington Cabernet and Merlot are consistently good.

Vintages to avoid (Oregon Pinot Noir) 1995.

Ten to try

With a few exceptions, Washington and Oregon wines are difficult to find outside the USA.

Red
- **Chateau Ste Michelle** Southern Slopes Cabernet Sauvignon, Washington ②
- **Adelsheim** Pinot Noir, Oregon ②
- **Columbia Crest** Merlot, Washington ②
- **Rex Hill** Pinot Noir, Oregon ③
- **L'École No.41** Merlot, Washington ④
- **Domaine Drouhin** Pinot Noir, Oregon ⑤
- **Andrew Will** Seven Hills Merlot, Washington ⑤

White
- **Columbia Crest** Chardonnay, Washington ②
- **Argyle** Dry Riesling, Oregon ②
- **Cooper Mountain** Pinot Gris, Oregon ②

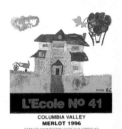

ABOVE *Velvety Merlot is the best of an excellent range of wines from Washington winery L'Ecole No. 41.* RIGHT *The Yakima Valley in Washington is in the rain shadow of the Cascade Mountains and its vineyards rely on irrigation.*

Can I afford them?

They're not cheap, compared to what's available from some other countries, particularly at the lower level. There's upwards pressure on price at the premium level, with producers seemingly competing to make the most expensive Cabernet or Chardonnay. Pinot Noir is about the price of its Burgundian equivalent; top Cabernet does not aim to be cheaper than top Bordeaux.

Washington and Oregon

These are newer wine regions than California, and still finding their feet by comparison. The two states make pretty distinct styles, with the Cascade Mountains forming a neat dividing line. On the western side of the mountains are the vineyards of Oregon, and a few stray vineyards belonging to Washington. Wines from here are light, with Pinot Noir in the silky, strawberryish style, understated, nutty Chardonnay, good spicy Pinot Gris, relatively neutral Pinot Blanc and the odd good Riesling.

Most of Washington State's vineyards are to the east of the Cascades and the wines are much richer in style. Pinot Noir gives way to Cabernet Sauvignon and Merlot in the intense, blackcurranty style; whites are ripe and toasty from Chardonnay and Semillon, and fairly tangy from Sauvignon Blanc. Rieslings, dry and sweet, are worth a look, too. And whereas Oregon has some real stars and a lot of wannabes, Washington State is more reliably good all round.

Do regions matter?

Each state has its star regions (the Dundee Hills in the Willamette Valley in Oregon; Yakima Valley and Walla Walla in Washington State), but quality depends more on the producer than the region.

Do vintages matter?

They matter more in Oregon than Washington and they matter most for Pinot Noir. See the Quick Guide, opposite.

Quick guide | New York State

Location New York State is the leading East Coast state for wine production.

Grapes The best European vines are Merlot and Pinot Noir for reds; Chardonnay and Riesling for whites. American or hybrid vines have very different flavours. They include Concord, Baco Noir, Chambourcin, Norton, Seyval Blanc and Vidal.

① Finger Lakes ② Long Island

Ten to try
New York wines are difficult to find outside the state.
  Red
• **Hargrave** Le Noirien Pinot Noir ②
• **Pellegrini** Cabernet Sauvignon ②
• **Paumanok** Assemblage ③
• **Bedell** Reserve Merlot ④

White
• **Glenora** Chardonnay ②
• **Lamoreaux Landing** Dry Riesling ②
• **Standing Stone** Riesling ②
• **Fox Run** Reserve Chardonnay ②
• **Gristina** Chardonnay ②
• **Hermann J Wiemer** Chardonnay ②

When do I drink them?

Any time. Washington reds are good food wines.

Can I afford them?

Oregon wines can never be cheap – conditions just aren't conducive to bulk production. But Washington can produce great flavours at a fair price.

New York State

The best wines here come from European vines like Merlot, Pinot Noir, Chardonnay and Riesling, but New York State has a long history of making wines using native vines and hybrids (crosses between American and European varieties), which can cope better with the harsh climate. The native vines belong to a different vine species from European varieties and have quite different flavours: strawberryish, but with an intense floral perfume.

Assuming we're talking only about European vines – well, quality is pretty good, and improving. Chardonnay is quite light and toasty; Riesling citrussy and flowery. Merlot tends to a grassy version of the juicy, fruity style rather than anything much more intense, but Pinot Noir is succulent and silky at best.

Do regions matter?

Long Island is the best, including the Hamptons and North Fork. The Finger Lakes are important, too.

Do vintages matter?

There is vintage variation here, but nearly all the wines are made to be drunk young.

When do I drink them?

Ideally, when holidaying in the Hamptons. Failing that, anytime will do.

Can I afford them?

Yes, but don't expect them to be bargain basement wines.

Other US wine regions

Virtually every state has some vines, mostly native American varieties. Much of the wine never makes it beyond the town line, let alone out of the state. However, winemakers in a wide range of locations are starting to get to grips with the demands of modern wine production for an international market.

Idaho in the west has some success with Riesling and Chardonnay. Over towards the East Coast, Pennsylvania, Maryland and Virginia make some decent wine from these grapes and also Sauvignon Blanc, Merlot and Cabernet Sauvignon. Down south in Texas you can find fruity Cabernet Sauvignon and attractive ripe Chardonnay and Sauvignon Blanc.

Quick guide | Canada

Location The vineyards are in the south, hugging the shores of the Great Lakes, and also near the Atlantic and Pacific coasts. See the map on page 116.

Grapes Pinot Noir, Merlot and hybrids for reds; Chardonnay, Pinot Gris and hybrids for whites; Riesling and Vidal for whites and icewine.

Local jargon *VQA* – the letters stand for *Vintners Quality Alliance*, an organisation which enforces high quality standards.

Ten to try
Canadian wines are difficult to find outside Canada.
White
- **Cave Spring** Dry Riesling 2
  - **Chateau des Charmes** Chardonnay 2
  - **Henry of Pelham** Reserve Chardonnay 2
  - **Burrowing Owl** Pinot Gris 2
- **Hillebrand Estates** Gewürztraminer 2
- **Lakeview** Riesling 2
- **Vineland Estates** Reserve Riesling 2
- **Mission Hill** Grand Reserve Barrel Select Chardonnay 2
Icewine
- **Inniskillin** 2
Red
- **Thirty Bench** Reserve Blend 2

LEFT AND RIGHT *The sweet, rich flavour of Canadian Icewine is a fair reward for the finger-numbing chill of the midwinter harvest.*

Canada

ICEWINE IS THE STAR here – sweet white made from grapes picked when the temperature plummets and freezes them on the vines. They are picked and pressed before they defrost, with the result that the water content stays behind in the press, and just the stickily sweet juice oozes out. It's a remarkable wine, made in tiny quantities from Riesling or Vidal grapes.

But of course it's not a wine you can drink every day. To make up for that, Canadian producers have been busy improving the quality of their dry wines, and they're now producing light, quite elegant flavours from classic cool-climate grapes. Pinot Noir and Merlot make pleasant, juicy reds; whites are nutty Chardonnay, mild, spicy Pinot Gris and crisp, citrussy Riesling. There are plenty of hybrid vines grown as well, for simple, perfumed, jammy reds and off-dry whites, but the best wines come from European vines.

Do regions matter?
The two major regions are the Niagara Peninsula in southern Ontario and the Okanagan Valley in British Columbia. Neither has a set style yet.

Do vintages matter?
They vary, but the wines are made to be drunk young. Red grapes don't always ripen; white grapes usually do.

When do I drink them?
The dry wines are good, light, all-purpose wines. Icewine should be savoured more slowly – though if you live in a European Union country you'll have to buy yourself an airline ticket first, as it cannot legally be imported into the EU due to some tedious legislation about alcohol levels.

Can I afford them?
Yes; they're reasonable value, though never that cheap.

South America

THE GREAT REVOLUTION in wine – the emergence of ripe, fruity reds and whites at prices everyone could afford – began in California in the 1970s and really took hold in Australia in the 1980s. But as the 20th century galloped to a close, South America had begun to mount a very serious challenge and was laying claim to becoming the most consumer-friendly region of the wine-producing world. The reasons were simple: fruit, flavour and value.

South American wine is the epitome of the modern New World style: flavours are soft and juicy for reds; clean, tangy or toasty for whites. Experimentation is the order of the day in the two major wine-exporting countries, Chile and Argentina, and some extremely serious wines are emerging alongside the excellent everyday bottles.

Brazil can produce some decent whites and together with Uruguay and its beefy, throbbing Tannat reds could yet provide a South American second division, but for now, for flavour and value, Chile and Argentina are a wine drinker's new best friends.

Chile

This is a country on the fast track to stardom. Chile has the good fortune to possess vast vineyards, free of disease, blessed with endless sunshine due to the rain shadow of the Andes – and equally blessed with endless supplies of irrigation water from those very same mountains. And the vineyards are stuffed full of classic grape varieties. Add all that to new-found political and economic stability and the 1990s were ripe for Chilean wine to burst onto the international stage.

Soft, juicy Merlot and Cabernet are what Chile is best known for in red wine, and toasty, tropically fruited Chardonnay and crisp, tangy Sauvignon Blanc in whites. But all sorts of other grape varieties are popping up: Syrah, Pinot Noir, Malbec, Carignan, Cinsaut, Carmenère, Sangiovese, Zinfandel and others for reds; Riesling, Semillon, Chenin Blanc, Gewürztraminer, Viognier and others for whites.

Reds share a basic style of ripe fruit and lots of it; whites are fresh and generally have good acidity, while aromatic grapes like Gewürztraminer and Viognier can be very highly perfumed. There's also a little deep-coloured rosé, with a light, strawberryish taste. Quality is utterly reliable. A few mega-priced reds have been launched, but these are more mixed in quality. Some are genuinely excellent, while others rely more on smart marketing.

Quick guide | Chile

Location The vineyards are predominantly in the Central Valley and its sub-regions Maipo, Rapel, Curicó and Maule. To the north is Aconcagua, which includes the important Casablanca Valley. To the south, the less highly regarded Southern Region includes the Itata and Bío-Bío sub-regions.

Santiago

① Aconcagua   ④ Curicó
② Maipo   ⑤ Maule
③ Rapel

Grapes Chile grows the whole range of international grapes. Merlot and Cabernet Sauvignon are the main reds; Chardonnay and Sauvignon Blanc the major whites. More than half of what was thought to be Merlot in Chile has recently turned out to be Carmenère (also known as Grande Vidure), which can produce attractively soft and juicy reds in much the same style as Merlot or deliciously rich, spicy yet savoury wines.

Ten to try
Red
- **Errázuriz** Merlot ②
- **Cono Sur** Reserve Pinot Noir ②

- **Viña Casablanca** Santa Isabel Estate Cabernet Sauvignon ②
- **Casa Lapostolle** Cuvée Alexandre Merlot ②
- **Montes** Alpha Syrah ②
- **Concha y Toro** Don Melchor Cabernet Sauvignon ③
- **Santa Rita** Casa Real Cabernet Sauvignon ④
White
- **La Palmería** Chardonnay Reserve ②
- **Viña Casablanca** Sauvignon Blanc ②
Rosé
- **Torres** Santa Digna Cabernet Sauvignon ②

ABOVE *Don Melchor is the top Cabernet from Concha y Toro, Chile's largest winery.* LEFT *Chile is no newcomer to wine production. The Errázuriz Panquehue vineyard in the Aconcagua Valley has thrived since 1870.*

Quick guide |
Argentina

Location Mendoza in central Argentina has by far the largest wine production. Salta in the extreme north and Rio Negro in the south are both upcoming quality wine regions. Other regions are San Juan and La Rioja in the north, and San Rafael in the south.

Grapes Red Malbec and white Torrontés are the main ones, but you'll also find Spain's red Tempranillo, the Italian red varieties Sangiovese, Barbera and Bonarda, and international favourites like Cabernet, Syrah and Chardonnay.

Ten to try
Red
- **Bodegas Balbi** Malbec ①
- **Santa Julia** Tempranillo ①
- **Norton** Sangiovese ①
- **Finca el Retiro** Syrah ②
- **Vallée de Vistalba** Cabernet Sauvignon ②
- **Humberto Canale** Malbec ②
- **Catena** Malbec ②
White
- **Bodegas J & F Lurton** Pinot Gris ①
- **Etchart** Torrontés ①
- **Michel Torino** Don David Torrontés ②

Argentina's vineyards stay close to the Andes. The high altitude keeps the temperature low and the mountains are also a vital source of water.

Do regions matter?

For whites, it's worth looking for the names of cool regions, Casablanca in particular.

Do vintages matter?

Not really, though cool regions like Casablanca have more vintage variation.

When do I drink them?

With friends, after work, with food, without food, any day, any time. Save the really expensive reds for impressing fans of red Bordeaux.

Can I afford them?

Easily, 99% of the time. For the other 1% of the wines you need to choose with care to get value for money.

Argentina

If Chilean wines are solidly international in style, Argentina is the place to go for flavour and value from grape varieties other than the New World staples of Cabernet Sauvignon, Merlot, Chardonnay and Sauvignon Blanc (although it does grow all of them, and very nice wines they make, too).

Malbec is Argentina's leading red grape, with flavours of wild herbs and spice as well as soft, juicy fruit; Argentina's white speciality is Torrontés, an aromatic, musky, sensuous wine. Successive waves of Spanish and Italian immigrants brought with them a huge selection of other grapes as well, and Argentine Barbera, Bonarda, Sangiovese and Tempranillo are all exciting, deliciously fruity red wines.

Argentina took longer than Chile to sort out its political and economic problems, and so it joined the international wine scene a few years later. Quality isn't yet as reliable as in Chile, but it's getting there rapidly and in the long run Argentina looks set to be the more interesting of the two.

Do regions matter?

Not yet. None has established a strong identity and the vast majority of Argentina's wine comes from the Mendoza region.

Do vintages matter?

No. In any case, the wines are mostly made to be drunk young.

When do I drink them?

Whenever you feel like something made nowhere else. Torrontés is a grape you'll be hard pushed to find in the rest of the world. Malbec grows in France (in Bordeaux and Cahors), and Barbera, Bonarda and Sangiovese in Italy, but never with these flavours.

Can I afford them?

Absolutely.

Other South American countries

Mexico suffers dry and fierce heat. With the aid of irrigation Baja California in the north and high-altitude vineyards further south make good sites for heat-loving red grapes. Powerful, rustic Cabernet Sauvignon and jammy Petite Sirah lead the way, but there's also Malbec, Grenache, Merlot, Zinfandel and Nebbiolo. White wines are not so good.

Brazil is South America's major wine producer after Argentina and Chile. Quantity is the main objective and its vineyards in the most tropical areas produce two harvests a year. White wines are most successful but generally dilute; reds are very light.

Uruguay has greater potential and does particularly well with wines made from the rare red grape Tannat, a variety from south-west France.

Peru throws most of its grapes into Pisco, the local brandy, but wine is produced in the southern region of Ica.

Bolivia again favours brandy, but does have some table wines made from Muscat. **Paraguay**, **Ecuador**, **Venezuela** and **Colombia** also make small quantities.

Australia

AUSTRALIA, AS YOU might expect from a land built by pioneers, is a wine pioneer as well. A nation that has had to make its own rules from the word go was never likely to be happy conforming to the norms of classic wine styles. And so it invented its own: upfront fruit, opulent texture and new oak, all at an affordable price. And it works equally well for reds and whites. European wines were the starting point, and the grapes (since Australia has no indigenous vines) are mainly the classic ones of Cabernet Sauvignon, Shiraz (France's Syrah), Chardonnay, Semillon and Riesling. But nowadays Australia has its own classic styles, and its influence (along with its well-trained wine-makers) has spread across Europe.

Because Australia is so different from Europe in the way it organises its wine industry, let's take a few moments to look at how it works. For one thing, every winemaking state in Australia makes almost every wine style. If you want a cool climate you go up into the hills, and further south; if you want a warm climate you go north, and stay nearer the plain. That way you can control whether your wines taste ripe, very ripe, or very ripe indeed. There's an increasing move to cool climates and more subtle wines; but Aussie wines never lose that ripeness. It's the single most important key to the national style.

Wines can come from a single vineyard, or they can be blended from every state in the country – or anything in between. Look at the distance involved – and then think of grapes being trucked perhaps from the Hunter Valley north of Sydney to the Barossa Valley near Adelaide, and arriving in perfect condition, ready to be made into ripe,

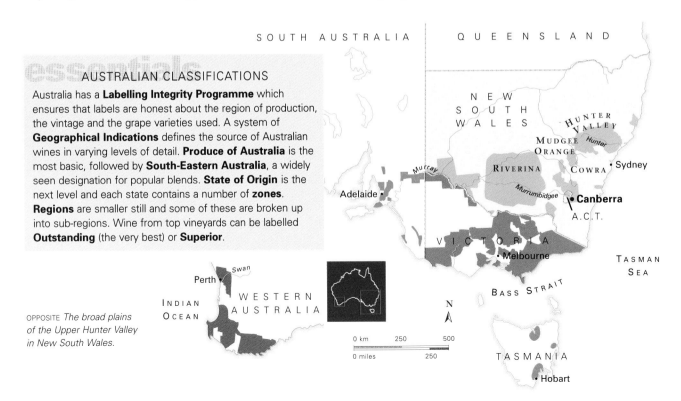

AUSTRALIAN CLASSIFICATIONS

Australia has a **Labelling Integrity Programme** which ensures that labels are honest about the region of production, the vintage and the grape varieties used. A system of **Geographical Indications** defines the source of Australian wines in varying levels of detail. **Produce of Australia** is the most basic, followed by **South-Eastern Australia**, a widely seen designation for popular blends. **State of Origin** is the next level and each state contains a number of **zones**. **Regions** are smaller still and some of these are broken up into sub-regions. Wine from top vineyards can be labelled **Outstanding** (the very best) or **Superior**.

OPPOSITE *The broad plains of the Upper Hunter Valley in New South Wales.*

fresh-tasting wines. That's the sort of technical know-how that Australia takes for granted.

Its winemakers are trained to produce tasty, clean, fruity wine in even the hottest, driest, most unpromising conditions – the sort of conditions that in Europe would in the past have been written off as incapable of making wine worth drinking. Australia changed all that with the introduction of refrigerated fermentation, for both whites and reds – the 20th century's single most important advance in winemaking technology. It's almost impossible to overstate Australia's influence on the flavour of the wine we drink.

New South Wales

New South Wales's strongest suit is its big, ripe wines, all fleshy and lush – the original Australian classics. The Hunter Valley and Cowra are the homes of this style;

Chardonnay is fat and full of tropical fruit and toast – the epitome of the ripe, toasty style – and Cabernet, too, especially from Mudgee, is rich and ripe, intensely blackcurranty and then some. Shiraz is rich, berried and leathery-tasting – spicy and warm-hearted on a big scale.

But the Hunter has another card to play: Semillon. This grape is found a lot in Bordeaux, where it is nearly always blended, both for dry and for sweet whites, with Sauvignon Blanc. Well, in the Hunter it stands alone in one of Australia's classic styles. When aged in new oak Semillon is ripe and toasty, full of lemon and lime fruit; when unoaked it is almost neutral when young, but ages to a wonderful toastiness, allied to waxy, lanolin richness and a flicker of nectarine sweetness.

Riverina is NSW's bulk wine area. Flavours here are generally fresh and simple, ripe and juicy, but there are oakier, more concentrated wines as well, and one or two world-class golden, super-sweet ones.

Quick guide | NSW

Location Lower and Upper
Hunter Valley, Mudgee,
Cowra, Orange and Riverina
are the major regions: see
the map on page 128.

Grapes Semillon and ripe,
toasty Chardonnay are the
whites; reds are spicy, warm-
hearted Shiraz and intense,
blackcurranty Cabernet.

Ten to try
Red
• **Reynolds** Shiraz ②
• **Brokenwood** Shiraz ③

• **Tyrrell's** Vat 9 Shiraz ④
• **Rosemount** Mountain
Blue Shiraz/Cabernet ⑤
White
• **Rothbury** Semillon ②
• **Brokenwood** Semillon ②
• **Allandale** Chardonnay ②
• **McWilliams** Elizabeth
Semillon ②
• **Rosemount Estate**
Orange Vineyard
Chardonnay ③
Sweet white
• **De Bortoli** Noble One
Botrytis Semillon ⑤

Quick guide | Victoria

Location Yarra Valley,
Rutherglen and Glenrowan
are the most significant
regions.

Grapes The stars are sweet
fortified Muscat and
Muscadelle (Tokay), and
subtle Pinot Noir and
Chardonnay.

Local jargon Rutherglen
Muscats come in four quality
grades. In ascending order,
they are: Rutherglen, Classic,
Grand and Rare.

Vintages to look for (Yarra)
1998, 1997, 1995, 1994,
1993, 1991, 1990.

Ten to try
Red
• **De Bortoli** Pinot Noir ③
• **Mount Langi Ghiran**
Shiraz ③
• **Yarra Yering** Dry Red
No. 1 ⑤

① Rutherglen and Glenrowan
② Yarra Valley

• **Mount Mary** Cabernets
Quintet ⑤
White
• **Chateau Tahbilk**
Marsanne ②
• **Delatite** Riesling ③
• **Tarrawarra** Chardonnay ④
Sparkling
• **Green Point** ③
• **Seppelt** Show Reserve
Sparkling Shiraz (red) ③
Fortified
• **Morris** Grand Rutherglen
Muscat ⑤

Do regions matter?

They do, but the producer usually matters more. Unoaked Semillon from the Hunter, however, is a unique style. Wines from Orange have a thrilling, lean intensity of fruit.

Do vintages matter?

Not that much except for reds from the Hunter.

When do I drink them?

Whenever you feel like fat, lush flavours. They can nearly all be drunk young; unoaked Semillon needs to age, but you don't need to build a cellar for the rest. When it comes to food, they want strong, clear flavours: throw a kangaroo steak on the barbie and off you go.

Can I afford them?

Mostly. The finer wines are expensive, but they're worth the money.

Victoria

Some of Australia's most individual wines come from here; and I'm talking about styles no other country in the world produces. These are Victoria's dark, warming, sweet fortified Muscats and Muscadelles (known locally as Tokays). They're nothing like port in flavour, although excellent port-style wines are made here – sherry styles, too. No, they are explosively sweet, with a concentrated grapiness and an intense perfume of coffee and toffee, raisins and nuts, and sometimes rose petals, that is almost shocking in its richness. The darkest, densest wines are almost treacly.

Victoria does cool-climate wines, too. It produces some of the country's tastiest Pinot Noir from the Yarra Valley. The best are a match for good Burgundy. Yarra Valley fizz is also excellent.

Other wines range from the inexpensive bulk wines from Murray Darling up to elegant reds and whites with well-defined flavours from the cooler areas near the coast. There are a few big, fat wines, but not as many as in NSW.

The cool hillsides of the Yarra Valley in Victoria produce the grapes for some of Australia's best sparkling wines and Pinot Noirs.

Do regions matter?

Yarra Valley has elegant wines with finely focused flavours: Chardonnay from here is more intense and nutty than rich and toasty. There are various small regions scattered around Melbourne. Mornington Peninsula and Geelong are fairly cool, but the climate gets warmer as you head north and the wines are correspondingly richer and beefier in the Goulburn Valley and Bendigo. Rutherglen and Glenrowan are the places for the fortified wines.

Do vintages matter?

In the Yarra and around Melbourne, yes. Elsewhere, not that much. See the Quick Guide, opposite.

When do I drink them?

Premium Yarra Valley reds and whites deserve a special occasion. The fortified Muscats are a match for chocolate, but you could also put them with – or on – ice cream, or just tuck into them on their own.

Can I afford them?

The best Yarra Valley Pinots are pretty expensive and suffer from vintage variations just as red Burgundies do. Fortified Muscats are quite expensive, especially the oldest ones, but they're certainly not overpriced.

South Australia

South Australia produces huge quantities of wine. It makes more than any other Australian state – everything from light wines to lush ones, from everyday cheapies to seriously expensive reds and whites. How to generalise? Impossible. Pick a style: chances are somebody's making it. Yes, there's the ubiquitous toasty Chardonnay, but South Australia has classic, unique styles, as well.

Barossa Valley Shiraz – often from very old vines, even a century old – is extraordinarily dense, spicy wine oozing sun-baked fruit: expect ripe tannins and flavours redolent of old leather, spices, earth, blackberries. McLaren Vale Shiraz is similar. And Grenache, again from very old vines, can be a riot of herbal, sweet-fruited flavours.

Rieslings from the Clare and Eden Valleys have established a new benchmark style for the grape. They're not a bit like either German or Alsace Rieslings: instead, they have a flavour of toast and limes.

Coonawarra Cabernet is probably what all Cabernet Sauvignon would taste like if it could: intense and blackcurranty, yes, but with a vivid brightness of fruit that is hard to find elsewhere, and a glorious minty edge.

Do regions matter?

They do, but it's a horribly complex picture. Wines from the Adelaide Hills are generally cool-climate and pinging

Quick guide | South Australia

Location The high-quality wines come from Barossa Valley, Eden Valley, Clare Valley, Adelaide Hills, Southern Vales, Coonawarra and Padthaway. Riverland is the bulk-wine region.

Grapes Anything and everything. Classics are Shiraz, Cabernet Sauvignon and Riesling.

Local jargon Don't confuse South Australia with the more general South-Eastern Australia appellation.

① Clare Valley
② Barossa & Eden Valleys
③ Riverland
④ Coonawarra

Twenty to try
Red
- **Peter Lehmann** Grenache ①
- **D'Arenberg** The Footbolt Grenache/Shiraz ②
  - **St Hallett** Gamekeeper's Reserve ②
- **Penfolds** Bin 28 Kalimna Shiraz ②
  - **Tim Adams** The Fergus ②
  - **Wolf Blass** President's Selection Shiraz ③
  - **Lenswood** Pinot Noir ③
  - **Chateau Reynella** Basket Pressed Shiraz ③
  - **Penley Estate** Cabernet Sauvignon ③
- **Rockford** Basket Press Shiraz ③
- **Hollick** Ravenswood Cabernet Sauvignon ⑤

White
- **Penfolds** Bin 202 Riesling ①
- **Wynns** Coonawarra Riesling ①
- **Yalumba** Oxford Landing Sauvignon Blanc ①
- **Tim Adams** Semillon ②
- **Shaw & Smith** Unoaked Chardonnay ②
- **Grosset** Polish Hill Riesling ③
- **Petaluma** Chardonnay ③
- **Mountadam** Chardonnay ③
  South-Eastern Australia
- **Lindemans** Bin 65 Chardonnay ① (a classic South-Eastern Australia budget blend)

ABOVE *Australia's premium Shiraz is Penfolds Grange, made using the very best grapes from numerous vineyards.*
RIGHT *Barossa is more than a wine region, it is also Australia's major centre for blending and bottling wine.*

with fruit; Barossa wines are bigger and beefier; and Coonawarra, Clare and Eden go for intensity without brawn. Other regions, including bulk-producer Riverland, deliver big, ultra-ripe flavours.

Do vintages matter?
Not really.

When do I drink them?
Drink Coonawarra Cabernets with a lunch of lamb roasted with garlic and rosemary. Hefty Barossa Shiraz is more of an evening wine. Clare and Eden Rieslings are ideal for quenching your thirst as the sun goes down. As for the Grenache, drink it when you want to go wild.

Can I afford them?
Absolutely. There are plenty of inexpensive, tasty wines. The best aren't cheap, but they are Australian classics. You should drink them once in a while to remind yourself of how amazing wine can be.

Western Australia

Here there's everything from fat, rich wines to elegant, restrained ones. The best wines have good structure and plenty of complexity. Quality is good to excellent.

Do regions or vintages matter?
Margaret River, Great Southern and Pemberton have cool climates and sleek wine. Swan District is hot. Vintages are pretty reliable.

When do I drink them?
Any time, though the best are worthy of very good food and a sense of occasion.

Can I afford them?
There are fewer inexpensive wines from here than from, say, South Australia. But you get good value at every level.

Tasmania

These are the lightest, crispest wines in all Australia. There also aren't many of them, and high production costs mean that they can never be cheap. But there's delicate Pinot Noir here, with surprisingly intense fruit, elegant Chardonnay and Riesling and very good sparkling wine.

Do regions or vintages matter?
The producer's name is the most important thing.

When do I drink them?
Any time.

Can I afford them?
They're never cheap. But they can be good.

Quick guide | Western Australia

Location See the map on page 128. The best regions are Margaret River, Great Southern and Pemberton. Swan District near Perth is the bulk region.

Grapes The usual Cabernet Sauvignon, Shiraz, Chardonnay, Riesling and Sauvignon Blanc, plus whites Chenin Blanc and Verdelho.

Five to try
Red
- **Moss Wood** Pinot Noir 3
- **Cullen** Cabernet/Merlot 4
- **Howard Park** Cabernet/ Merlot 5
White
- **Cape Mentelle** Semillon/ Sauvignon Blanc 2
- **Leeuwin Estate** Chardonnay 5

Quick guide | Tasmania

Location The island state of Tasmania is the most southerly, and coolest and wettest, part of Australia. See the map on page 128.

Grapes Intense, nutty Chardonnay whites and silky, strawberryish Pinot Noir reds – and sparkling wine made from both; also some grassy, blackcurranty Cabernet.

Five to try
Tasmanian wines are difficult to find outside Australia.
Red
- **Freycinet** Pinot Noir 3
- **Domaine A** Pinot Noir 3
White
- **Moorilla** Chardonnay 3
- **Pipers Brook** Riesling 3
Sparkling
- **Pipers Brook** Pirie 4

New Zealand

THIS IS THE HOME of benchmark New World Sauvignon Blanc, the archtypal green, tangy wine. And it's a pretty recent benchmark, too, because the first Sauvignon Blanc was planted in Marlborough – now a classic region for the grape – in 1973. It became clear almost instantly that this is what Sauvignon Blanc should taste like. Until then the only benchmark for the grape had been Sancerre and the other Sauvignons of the Loire Valley. New Zealand Sauvignon is more aggressive, more gooseberryish, more pungent, whereas Sancerre is rounder, more subtle – and more unreliable. Sauvignon Blanc in New Zealand, at whatever level of quality, has that hallmark gooseberry fruit. It's almost irresistibly mouthwatering.

But New Zealand is not all Sauvignon Blanc. Generally speaking it makes cool-climate New World styles that are lighter and leaner than Australian wines, and it is good at grapes Australia finds more difficult, in particular subtle, mellow Pinot Noir. There's good nutty Chardonnay, as well as toastier, fruitier styles, floral Riesling and excellent Champagne-style sparkling wine. It also grows Cabernet Sauvignon and Merlot, but they tend to taste a bit green-leafy rather than fruity – especially the Cabernet.

Do regions matter?
The climate varies from the north of the North Island, where it's very warm, to the south of the South Island, where it's distinctly chilly, and climate is the key to what grows where in New Zealand. The most important regions are Marlborough for Sauvignon Blanc and fizz, Hawke's Bay for Cabernet and Merlot, and Martinborough for Pinot Noir. Chardonnay grows pretty much everywhere.

Do vintages matter?
They do, but few wines repay aging. Buy wines from a recent year and drink them young.

When do I drink them?
Anytime. Cult Sauvignon Blancs like Cloudy Bay will impress your wine buff friends.

Can I afford them?
New Zealand wines are never going to be the cheapest to make, and most producers, realising this, go for quality. It's worth spending a bit more and getting something extra good.

South Africa

SOUTH AFRICA was a relatively late starter in the international wine stakes. It's been on a steep learning curve since the demise of the Apartheid regime in the early 1990s and its subsequent emergence from international isolation. But year by year it's catching up.

It makes all possible styles, from green and tangy whites, through broad-beamed, nutty whites, to rich toasty ones; and reds from light and juicy Cinsauts, through strawberry-soft Pinot Noirs and challenging, blackcurranty Cabernets to spicy, booming Shiraz and Pinotage. There are fortifieds, too, both light and dry sherry-like ones and sweet, dark ones in the style of port.

The range of grapes encompasses all the international favourites – Cabernet Sauvignon, Merlot, Chardonnay, Sauvignon Blanc – and there's Chenin Blanc as well, mostly used for everyday whites. But carefully made Chenin from old vines is good stuff and could be a future star in the Cape. The country's speciality is the Pinotage grape,

Quick guide | New Zealand

Location The most southerly of the southern hemisphere wine countries.

Grapes Sauvignon Blanc, Chardonnay, Riesling (sweet and dry) and Gewürztraminer are the grapes for the best whites; Müller-Thurgau is decidedly inferior. Pinot Noir, the Cabernets and Merlot are the reds. Styles vary from north to south. Hawke's Bay Sauvignon Blanc is softer and riper than the tangy, gooseberryish Marlborough style. Chardonnay is richer in the north. Pinot Noir likes cool Martinborough and Otago, but Cabernet and Merlot are happier in the north.

Ten to try

Red
- **Corbans** North Island Merlot ②
- **Martinborough Vineyards** Pinot Noir ③

White
- **Giesen** Dry Riesling ②
- **Villa Maria** Private Bin Sauvignon Blanc ②
- **Palliser Estate** Sauvignon Blanc ②
- **Montana** 'O' Ormond Estate Chardonnay ③
- **Kumeu River** Chardonnay ③
- **Cloudy Bay** Sauvignon Blanc ③

Sparkling
- **Deutz** Cuvée Marlborough ③
- **Cloudy Bay** Pelorus ③

① Auckland
② Gisborne
③ Hawke's Bay
④ Wairarapa (including Martinborough)
⑤ Nelson
⑥ Marlborough
⑦ Canterbury
⑧ Central Otago

0 km   200
0 miles   200

CLOUDY BAY

LEFT *The breathtaking view from Rippon Vineyard in Otago is a constant reminder of the region's cool climate.* ABOVE *Another dramatic vineyard location inspired the label of Cloudy Bay – probably New Zealand's most famous wine.*

N

① Olifants River
② Paarl
③ Stellenbosch
④ Robertson
⑤ Overberg

Olifants

Cape Town

0 km   200

0 miles   200

Quick guide | South Africa

Location Virtually all the wine regions are clustered around Cape Town in the south-west of the country. Paarl and Stellenbosch, districts of the vast Coastal Region, are the best established. Robertson is good for Chardonnay. Overberg (including Walker Bay) in the far south has a cooler climate and is promising for Pinot Noir. Olifants River is a bulk wine-producing region.

Grapes Pinotage is South Africa's own red grape. Cabernet Sauvignon and Merlot are popular. Syrah/Shiraz and other Rhône reds, and even California's Zinfandel, are joining the repertoire. Chardonnay and Sauvignon Blanc are both widely grown whites and there's also some Riesling. Chenin Blanc is used for the simplest whites and a few high-quality ones.

Local jargon *Wine of Origin (WO)* – this seal at the top of the bottle guarantees the wine's area of origin, grape variety or varieties and vintage. *Estate wine* – wine that is grown and made on a registered estate, usually a sign of good quality.

Ten to try
Red
- **Fairview** Cabernet Sauvignon ②
- **Kaapzicht** Shiraz ②
- **Warwick** Traditional Old Bush Vine Pinotage ②
- **Bouchard Finlayson** Pinot Noir ③
- **Kanonkop** Pinotage ③
- **Hamilton Russell** Pinot Noir ③

White
- **Buitenverwachting** Riesling ②
- **L'Avenir** Chenin Blanc ②
- **Glen Carlou** Reserve Chardonnay ③
- **Thelema** Sauvignon Blanc ③

The Drakensberg mountains dwarf the 17th-century manor house of the Boschendal vineyard in Paarl.

which makes both light reds and seriously heavyweight ones. It has a flamboyant toasted marshmallow and damson flavour that is unique and thrilling at its best.

Quality in South Africa is still uneven compared to Chile or Australia – countries with which it is competing on the international market. Flavours can be a bit too stolid, less instantly appealing, and reds often have a raw green sting in their tail. But they're getting there.

Do regions matter?
Yes and no. Some cool areas like Constantia to the south of Cape Town and Walker Bay in Overberg are making very individual styles, but the bulk of the wines come from warmer and more consistent regions like Paarl, Stellenbosch and Robertson.

Do vintages matter?
Not for the majority of wines.

When do I drink them?
Anytime, but the reds are best with food.

Can I afford them?
They're seldom the greatest value in the New World, but Chenin Blanc is always cheap and sometimes excellent. Pinotage and Shiraz are usually good value for money.

Other wine-producing countries

Eastern Mediterranean
Lebanon's finest producers by miles are Chateau Musar and Kefraya, with world-class spicy, chocolaty reds. Israel makes good international styles from Cabernet Sauvignon, Chardonnay and others. Cyprus is constantly said to be on the brink of producing good wine, yet we never quite seem to see it.

Africa
Zimbabwe has a fledgling wine industry with modern ideas and international ambitions. It's growing all the serious grapes and Chardonnay looks promising. North African wine is in decline. The massive growth of the vineyards of Morocco, Tunisia and Algeria in the past was fuelled by the need of France, the colonial power, for cheap, alcoholic reds. Now they have no real market. The wines are tough, solid and old-fashioned.

Asia
Indigenous enthusiasm and serious Western investment are the keys to opening up the potential of regions of India, China and Japan.

Wines from Lebanon, China and India testify to the worldwide interest in developing ancient or previously untried wine regions. Who knows how the map of the world of wine will change in years to come?

Appellation decoder

The trouble with buying European wines is that many are named according to where they come from – the appellation – rather than what's in them: the grape variety or varieties. And if you have heard of a wine but aren't sure exactly which region the appellation is in, it can be a hassle to find it in a shop or on a wine list. To help you sort things out this table brings together appellations, their major styles, their regions and their key grape varieties.

KEY ♟ Red ♟ White

Name	♟/♟	Region	Major Grape Varieties
ALOXE-CORTON	♟	Côte de Beaune, Burgundy, France	*Pinot Noir*
ASTI (sweet/sparkling)	♟	Piedmont, North-west Italy	*Muscat (called Moscato here)*
BAIRRADA	♟	Portugal	*Baga*
BANDOL	♟	Provence, France	*Mourvèdre/Grenache/Cinsaut*
BARBARESCO	♟	Piedmont, North-west Italy	*Nebbiolo*
BARDOLINO	♟	Veneto, North-east Italy	*Corvina*
BAROLO	♟	Piedmont, North-west Italy	*Nebbiolo*
BEAUJOLAIS	♟	Burgundy, France	*Gamay*
BEAUNE	♟	Côte de Beaune, Burgundy, France	*Pinot Noir*
BERGERAC	♟/♟	South-West France	♟ *Cabernet Sauvignon & Franc/ Merlot;* ♟ *Sémillon/Sauvignon Blanc*
BONNEZEAUX (sweet)	♟	Loire Valley, France	*Chenin Blanc*
BOURGUEIL	♟	Loire Valley, France	*Cabernet Franc*
BROUILLY/CÔTE DE BROUILLY	♟	Beaujolais, Burgundy, France	*Gamay*
BRUNELLO DI MONTALCINO	♟	Tuscany, Central Italy	*Sangiovese*
CAHORS	♟	South-West France	*Malbec/Merlot/Tannat*
CHABLIS	♟	Burgundy, France	*Chardonnay*
CHAMBOLLE-MUSIGNY	♟	Côte de Nuits, Burgundy, France	*Pinot Noir*
CHAMPAGNE (sparkling)	♟	Champagne, France	*Chardonnay/Pinot Noir/Pinot Meunier*
CHASSAGNE-MONTRACHET	♟/♟	Côte de Beaune, Burgundy, France	♟ *Pinot Noir;* ♟ *Chardonnay*
CHÂTEAUNEUF-DU-PAPE	♟/♟	Southern Rhône Valley, France	♟ *Grenache/Syrah;* ♟ *Roussanne*
CHÉNAS	♟	Beaujolais, Burgundy, France	*Gamay*
CHIANTI	♟	Tuscany, Central Italy	*Sangiovese*
CHIROUBLES	♟	Beaujolais, Burgundy, France	*Gamay*
CONDRIEU	♟	Northern Rhône Valley, France	*Viognier*
CORBIÈRES	♟	Languedoc-Roussillon, France	*Carignan/Grenache/Cinsaut*
CORNAS	♟	Northern Rhône Valley, France	*Syrah*
COSTIÈRES DE NÎMES	♟	Languedoc-Roussillon, France	*Carignan/Grenache/Mourvèdre/Syrah*

Name	🍷/🥂	Region	Major Grape Varieties
CÔTE DE NUITS-VILLAGES	🍷	Côte de Nuits, Burgundy, France	*Pinot Noir*
CÔTE-RÔTIE	🍷	Northern Rhône Valley, France	*Syrah*
COTEAUX DU LANGUEDOC	🍷	Languedoc-Roussillon, France	*Carignan/Grenache*
COTEAUX DU LAYON	(sweet) 🥂	Loire Valley, France	*Chenin Blanc*
CÔTES DU ROUSSILLON	🍷	Languedoc-Roussillon, France	*Carignan/Cinsaut/Grenache*
CROZES-HERMITAGE	🍷/🥂	Northern Rhône Valley, France	🍷 *Syrah;* 🥂 *Marsanne/Roussanne*
DÃO	🍷	Portugal	*Touriga Nacional/Tinta Roriz (Tempranillo)*
DÔLE	🍷	Switzerland	*Pinot Noir/Gamay*
ENTRE-DEUX-MERS	🥂	Bordeaux, France	*Sémillon/Sauvignon Blanc*
FAUGÈRES	🍷	Languedoc-Roussillon, France	*Carignan/Grenache/Syrah*
FITOU	🍷	Languedoc-Roussillon, France	*Carignan/Cinsaut/Grenache*
FLEURIE	🍷	Beaujolais, Burgundy, France	*Gamay*
FRASCATI	🥂	Lazio, Central Italy	*Malvasia/Trebbiano*
GAVI	🥂	Piedmont, North-west Italy	*Cortese*
GEVREY-CHAMBERTIN	🍷	Côte de Nuits, Burgundy, France	*Pinot Noir*
GIGONDAS	🍷	Southern Rhône Valley, France	*Grenache*
GIVRY	🍷	Côte Chalonnaise, Burgundy, France	*Pinot Noir*
GRAVES	🍷/🥂	Bordeaux, France	🍷 *Cabernet Sauvignon & Franc/ Merlot;* 🥂 *Sémillon/Sauvignon Blanc*
HERMITAGE	🍷/🥂	Northern Rhône Valley, France	🍷 *Syrah;* 🥂 *Marsanne/Roussanne*
JULIÉNAS	🍷	Beaujolais, Burgundy, France	*Gamay*
LISTRAC	🍷	Haut-Médoc, Bordeaux, France	*Cabernet Sauvignon & Franc/Merlot*
MÂCON/MÂCON-VILLAGES	🥂	Mâconnais, Burgundy, France	*Chardonnay*
MARGAUX	🍷	Haut-Médoc, Bordeaux, France	*Cabernet Sauvignon & Franc/Merlot*
MÉDOC/HAUT-MÉDOC	🍷	Bordeaux, France	*Cabernet Sauvignon & Franc/Merlot*
MERCUREY	🍷/🥂	Côte Chalonnaise, Burgundy, France	🍷 *Pinot Noir;* 🥂 *Chardonnay*
MEURSAULT	🥂	Côte de Beaune, Burgundy, France	*Chardonnay*
MINERVOIS	🍷	Languedoc-Roussillon, France	*Grenache/Syrah/Mourvèdre*
MONTAGNY	🥂	Côte Chalonnaise, Burgundy, France	*Chardonnay*
MOREY-ST-DENIS	🍷	Côte de Nuits, Burgundy, France	*Pinot Noir*
MORGON	🍷	Beaujolais, Burgundy, France	*Gamay*
MOULIN-À-VENT	🍷	Beaujolais, Burgundy, France	*Gamay*
MOULIS	🍷	Haut-Médoc, Bordeaux, France	*Cabernet Sauvignon & Franc/Merlot*
MUSCADET	🥂	Loire Valley, France	*Melon de Bourgogne*
NUITS-ST-GEORGES	🍷	Côte de Nuits, Burgundy, France	*Pinot Noir*
ORVIETO	🥂	Umbria, Central Italy	*Trebbiano*
PAUILLAC	🍷	Haut-Médoc, Bordeaux, France	*Cabernet Sauvignon & Franc/Merlot*

Name	♟/♟	Region	Major Grape Varieties
PESSAC-LÉOGNAN	♟/♟	Bordeaux, France	♟ Cabernet Sauvignon & Franc/ Merlot; ♟ Sémillon/Sauvignon Blanc
POMEROL	♟	Bordeaux, France	Merlot/Cabernet Sauvignon & Franc
POMMARD	♟	Côte de Beaune, Burgundy, France	Pinot Noir
POUILLY- FUISSÉ	♟	Mâconnais, Burgundy, France	Chardonnay
POUILLY-FUMÉ	♟	Loire Valley, France	Sauvignon Blanc
POUILLY-SUR-LOIRE	♟	Loire Valley, France	Chasselas
PRIORAT	♟	Spain	Garnacha (Grenache)
PULIGNY-MONTRACHET	♟	Côte de Beaune, Burgundy, France	Chardonnay
QUARTS DE CHAUME	(sweet)♟	Loire Valley, France	Chenin Blanc
RÉGNIÉ	♟	Beaujolais, Burgundy, France	Gamay
RÍAS BAIXAS	♟	Spain	Albariño
RIBERA DEL DUERO	♟	Spain	Tempranillo (called Tinto Fino here)
RIOJA	♟/♟	Spain	♟ Tempranillo/Garnacha (Grenache); ♟ Viura
RULLY	♟/♟	Côte Chalonnaise, Burgundy, France	♟ Pinot Noir; ♟ Chardonnay
ST-AMOUR	♟	Beaujolais, Burgundy, France	Gamay
ST-CHINIAN	♟	Languedoc-Roussillon, France	Carignan/Cinsaut/Grenache
ST-ÉMILION	♟	Bordeaux, France	Merlot/Cabernet Sauvignon & Franc
ST-ESTÈPHE	♟	Haut-Médoc, Bordeaux, France	Cabernet Sauvignon & Franc/Merlot
ST-JOSEPH	♟/♟	Northern Rhône Valley, France	♟ Syrah; ♟ Marsanne/Roussanne
ST-JULIEN	♟	Haut-Médoc, Bordeaux, France	Cabernet Sauvignon & Franc/Merlot
ST-NICOLAS-DE-BOURGUEIL	♟	Loire Valley, France	Cabernet Franc
ST-VÉRAN	♟	Mâconnais, Burgundy, France	Chardonnay
SANCERRE	♟/♟	Loire Valley, France	♟ Sauvignon Blanc; ♟ Pinot Noir
SAUMUR-CHAMPIGNY	♟	Loire Valley, France	Cabernet Franc & Sauvignon
SAUTERNES	(sweet)♟	Bordeaux, France	Sémillon/Sauvignon Blanc
SAVENNIÈRES	♟	Loire Valley, France	Chenin Blanc
SOAVE	♟	Veneto, North-east Italy	Garganega/Trebbiano
TORO	♟	Spain	Tempranillo (called Tinto del Toro here)
VACQUEYRAS	♟	Southern Rhône Valley, France	Grenache/Syrah/Mourvèdre
VALPOLICELLA	♟	Veneto, North-east Italy	Corvina
VINO NOBILE DI MONTEPULCIANO	♟	Tuscany, Central Italy	Sangiovese
VOLNAY	♟	Côte de Beaune, Burgundy, France	Pinot Noir
VOSNE-ROMANÉE	♟	Côte de Nuits, Burgundy, France	Pinot Noir
VOUGEOT	♟	Côte de Nuits, Burgundy, France	Pinot Noir
VOUVRAY	♟	Loire Valley, France	Chenin Blanc

The most useful words in wine

Acidity Acid, naturally present in grapes, gives wine its intense and refreshing qualities.

Appellation An officially designated place of origin. In Europe many wines have to be made from a specified grape variety or varieties to qualify for the appellation name.

Barrel aging Time spent maturing in wood, often 225-litre oak barrels called **barriques**. The wine takes on oak flavours from the wood.

Barrel-fermented Describes wine fermented in oak barrels. Like barrel aging, this process gives the wine characteristic oak flavours.

Blend Mixture of wines of different grapes, styles, origin or age. Blending is carried out to improve the balance of the wine, or to maintain a consistent style.

Botrytis or **(noble rot)** A fungus which sometimes attacks grapes, reducing the water content and concentrating the sugar and acidity. Botrytised grapes are ideal for making intense golden, sweet wines such as Sauternes.

Cépage Simply the French word for a grape variety.

Climate A critical influence on the style and quality of wine. Cool climate areas such as Germany, Champagne and Oregon are at the coolest limits for grape ripening and are good for reserved, elegant styles. In warm-climate areas vines ripen easily but often need to be irrigated. Warm-climate wines are rich and high in alcohol. Red grapes generally need a warmer climate than white grapes.

Cold fermentation Long, slow fermentation at low temperature to extract freshness and fruit flavour from the grapes. Crucial for white wines in warm climates.

Corked Term used to describe wine tainted by a contaminated cork. Corked wine has a mouldy, musty smell.

Cru French term meaning 'growth', used to refer to the wine of an individual vineyard and often in conjunction with a quality ranking, such as Premier Cru (First Growth).

Cuvée Literally the contents of a *cuve* or vat. The term refers to a particular blend, either of different grape varieties or of wine from selected barrels and is used to distinguish, for example, a producer's top Chardonnay and everyday Chardonnay.

Domaine A wine estate, particularly in Burgundy.

Dry A wine that is not perceptibly sweet.

Enologist A wine scientist.

Estate-bottled A wine made and bottled by a single property, though this may encompass several different vineyards. Equivalent terms are **mis en bouteille au château/domaine** in French, **azienda agricola** or **imbottigliato all'origine** in Italian and **Erzeugerabfüllung** or **Gutsabfüllung** in German.

Fermentation The process of transforming sugar into alcohol.

Late-harvest or **vendange tardive** (France) Wine made from super-ripe grapes picked after the normal harvest. Late-harvest wines are usually sweet.

Malolactic fermentation A natural process which turns harsh malic acid in a wine into softer-tasting lactic acid. Malolactic fermentation is prevented in many white wines to preserve the refreshing bite.

Négociant French term for a merchant or shipper who buys wine or grapes from growers, then matures, maybe blends and bottles the wine for sale.

New World The non-European wine-producing countries that have come to the world's attention since the 1970s. The United States, Australia, New Zealand, South America and South Africa are all New World countries. New World is also an attitude of mind that embraces new technology in the attempt to produce fresher, fruitier wines.

Noble rot *See* botrytis.

Oak Oak barrels contribute characteristic toasty vanilla flavours and a rounded taste to many wines. Oak chips dunked into the wine or even oak flavouring are cheaper alternatives.

Old vines or **vieilles vignes** (France) Mature vines producing grapes with intense flavours. There are no legal definitions of how old a vine has to be to qualify, but the term is a fairly reliable indicator of quality.

Old World The traditional wine-producing countries of Europe, home to most of the world's established wine styles and grape varieties. Old World can also refer to traditional techniques employed in other countries.

Producer The company that makes the wine and the most important consideration when choosing a wine. In the same region and the same vintage a good producer will make far better wine than a poor one, and the wine won't necessarily be any more expensive.

Reserva (Spain) and **riserva** (Italy) Legally defined terms for wines that receive extra aging either in oak barrels or in bottle (or both)

before they go on sale. These terms carry quality connotations. Elsewhere 'reserve' has no legal definition and does not necessarily indicate a higher quality of wine.

Residual sugar Sugar left over in the wine after fermentation is complete. A perceptible level of residual sugar makes the wine taste sweet.

Single-vineyard Wines with real individuality tend to be made using grapes from just one vineyard.

Tannin The bitter, mouth-drying component in red wines, which is harsh when young but adds depth to the flavour and is crucial to a wine's ability to age.

Terroir The concept that wine is an expression of where it comes from, rather than simply a product of the climate and grape variety.

Varietal Wine made from, and named after, a single grape variety.

Vendange tardive *See* late-harvest.

Vieilles vignes *See* old vines.

Vinification The process of turning grapes into wine.

Vintage The year's grape harvest, also used to describe the wine of a particular year.

Viticulture Vine-growing and vineyard management.

Vitis vinifera The species of vine that all the classic grape varieties belong to.

Winemaker The person responsible for controlling the vinification process.

Yield Perhaps the most important factor in determining the quality of a wine. The lower the quantity of grapes each vine is allowed to produce, the more intense the juice in the grapes and the flavours in the wine will be.

Index

HWI LEARNING CENTRE

PICTURE CREDITS

Stephen Bartholomew: author photography 5, 26, 47, 49, 52–6, 66, 71, 72.
Cephas Picture Library: Kevin Argue 122–3; Andy Christodolo 135; Kevin Judd 29 top right, 43, 44, 45 left; M J Kielty 91; Herbert Lehmann 29 top left; R & K Muschenetz 25 top left, 39, 120, 125, 126; Alain Proust 136; Mick Rock 6, 23, 25 top right, bottom left, bottom right, 26, 27, 28, 29 bottom, 33, 34, 36, 37, 38, 40, 45 right, 75, 77, 81, 84, 86–7, 89, 93, 95, 97, 99, 102, 104–05, 106, 109, 110, 115, 117, 129, 131, 132; Ted Stefanski 31.
Robert Hall: 2–3, 7, 8–22, 46–7, 49 (corkscrews and corks), 50–1, 52 (glasses), 54 (inset), 57.
Stephen Marwood: bottle photography 35, 78, 95, 100, 115, 122, 132.
Roberson, London: 66.
Spiral Cellars Ltd: 65.
Zaika, London: 59.